Home Sweet Home
Paper Piecing

**Mix & Match 17 Paper-Pieced Blocks
7 Charming Projects**

Mary Hertel

C&T PUBLISHING
Another Maker Inspired!

Text copyright © 2023 by Mary Ann Hertel

Photography and artwork copyright © 2023 by C&T Publishing, Inc.

Publisher: Amy Barrett-Daffin

Creative Director: Gailen Runge

Senior Editor: Roxane Cerda

Editor: Liz Aneloski

Technical Editor: Debbie Rodgers

Cover/Book Designer: April Mostek

Production Coordinator: Zinnia Heinzmann

Illustrator: Aliza Shalit

Photography Coordinator: Lauren Herberg and Gailen Runge

Photography Assistant: Rachel Ackley

Subject and lifestyle photography by Lauren Herberg for C&T Publishing Inc.; instructional photography by C&T Publishing, Inc., unless otherwise noted

Published by C&T Publishing, Inc., P.O. Box 1456, Lafayette, CA 94549

Library of Congress Cataloging-in-Publication Data

Names: Hertel, Mary, 1955- author.
Title: Home sweet home paper piecing : mix & match 17 paper-pieced blocks, 7 charming projects / Mary Hertel.
Description: Lafayette, CA : C&T Publishing, [2023] | Summary: "In Home Sweet Home Paper Piecing, Readers will find 17 bestselling and new paper pieced blocks featuring fun and engaging gnomes, animals, and a flower all able to mix and match into 7 brand new projects to decorate your home or give as gifts"-- Provided by publisher.
Identifiers: LCCN 2023004190 | ISBN 9781644033791 (trade paperback) | ISBN 9781644033807 (ebook)
Subjects: LCSH: Patchwork--Patterns. | Sewing.
Classification: LCC TT835 .H44675 2023 | DDC 746.46/041--dc23/eng/20230217
LC record available at https://lccn.loc.gov/2023004190

Printed in China

10 9 8 7 6 5 4 3 2 1

Dedication I dedicate this book to paper piecing instructors around the world. Sewing and quilting are life skills that benefit others. I hope this book will be helpful to teachers and students everywhere.

Acknowledgments Thank you to the C&T Publishing editors. You push me to execute my best patterns and projects.

Contents

Lap Quilt   12

Baby Quilt   18

Oversized Floor Pillow   22

Pillowcase   28

Wall Hanging   38

Table Runner   36

Tote with Zipper   41

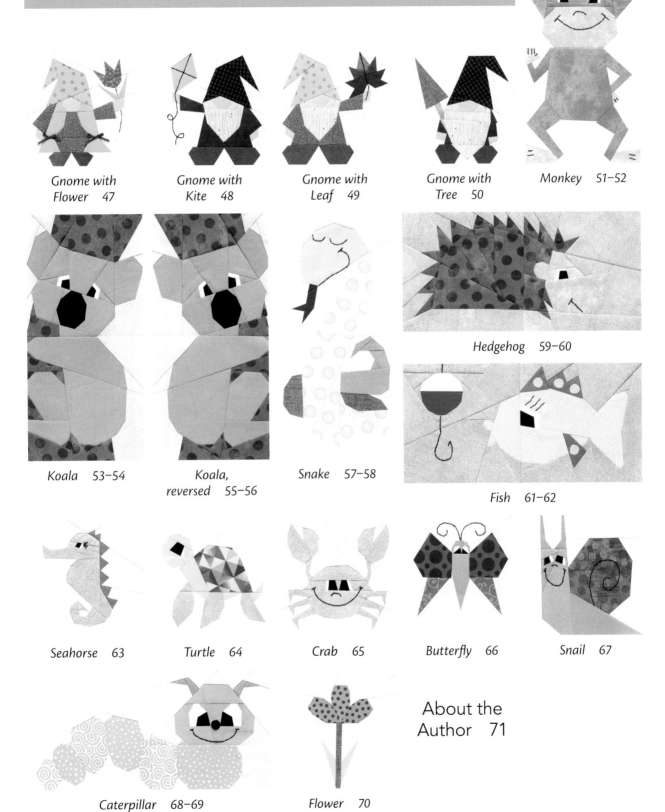

Introduction

Would you love to create my favorite paper pieced blocks? This book is filled with designs that make me smile. I have enjoyed creating them, and I hope you enjoy sewing them into lovely household items. Get ready to create gifts for yourself and others that reach a whole new level. You will find full patterns for quilts, a table runner, a wall hanging, a tote, and more!

This book includes step-by-step instructions for paper piecing (see Paper Piecing Basics, next page), 7 beautiful home decor projects, and 17 of my favorite block patterns. Some of the blocks are 8″ × 8″ squares, and some are a combination of two square blocks 8″ × 8″ sewn together, which result in a rectangular block that is 8″ × 15½″.

As in all of my previous books, the block patterns are interchangeable in all of the projects. That means you can conceivably create hundreds of projects using my books. Plus, these blocks will also fit into the projects from my previous six books, which means you can be super creative!

Let's start paper piecing these fun blocks. Everything you need to know is right here!

Photo by Gail Cameron

Paper Piecing Basics

Tools

- Paper (I use Carol Doak's Foundation Paper by C&T Publishing)
- Sharp scissors
- Rotary cutter and mat
- Ruler with an easy-to-read ¼" line (such as Add-A-Quarter ruler by CM Designs)
- Multipurpose tool (such as Alex Anderson's 4-in-1 Essential Sewing Tool by C&T Publishing) or seam ripper.
- Flat-head straight pins
- Lamp or light source (window)
- Sewing machine
- Iron and pressing board

Things To Know

STITCH LENGTH

Set the stitch length at 1.5, which is about 20 stitches per inch. The stitch perforations must be close together to allow the paper to rip easily, but not so close that ripping out a seam is an impossible task.

PREPARE A CONVENIENT WORK STATION

Have the iron, pressing board, and cutting mat close to the sewing machine. There should be a light source handy for positioning scrap pieces on the back of the pattern. A window works well during the day and a lamp at night.

THE BUTTERFLY EFFECT

After sewing a seam line, the fabric is flipped behind the numbered piece on the pattern that you are currently attaching. This creates a butterfly effect, meaning that the fabric scrap needs to be lined up to the seam in such a way that it will cover the space you are sewing after it is flipped into place. If you are concerned that the size of your scrap is insufficient, pin along the seam line and try flipping the scrap into place before sewing the seam. That way, if the scrap does not cover the area sufficiently, you can adjust it or find a larger scrap.

FOLLOW ALONG
If you are new to paper piecing, follow along for practice using the Hedgehog block (page 59) as you read the following instructions.

Preparing the Patterns

1 Make the recommended number of color copies of the original block. (You need 4 copies for the Hedgehog, Part 1 block.)

2 Cut the block into the segments denoted by the capital letters, *adding ¼" seam allowances along the red lines and the outside edges of the block*. For the example, use one copy for Segments A and E, and one copy each for Segments B, C, and D.

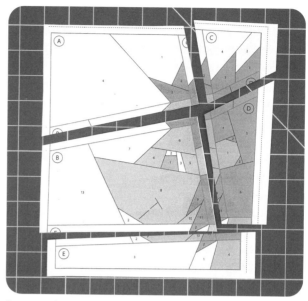

Segments A, B, C, D, and E with ¼" seam allowances around outside edges

Paper Piecing A Segment

Always stitch pieces in numerical order. Don't forget to set your stitch length (page 7) to 1.5, or about 20 stitches per inch.

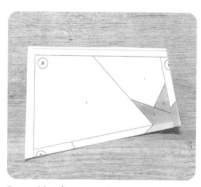

Front side of segment A

1 Pin the *wrong* side of the Piece 1 fabric onto the *unprinted* side of the paper pattern. The right side of the fabric faces you (away from the paper).

Note: In this example, I am substituting a turquoise background for the white background shown in the pattern.

2 Bend the paper pattern and fabric along the seamline between Pieces 1 and 2. Use a heavy piece of tag board, such as a bookmark or postcard, to make the fold. This will help you line up the fabric for Piece 2.

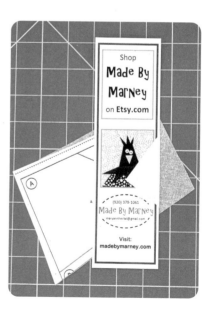

3 Use the Add-A-Quarter ruler to trim the fabric behind Piece 1 to ¼".

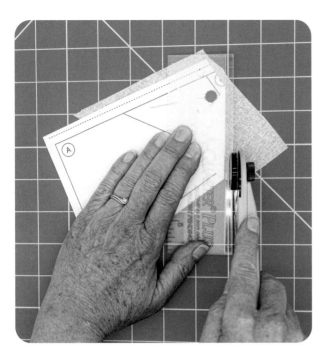

4 Keeping the pattern bent back along the seam line, align the Piece 2 fabric with the fabric from Piece 1 right sides together. The fabric for Piece 2 will be flipped into place after sewing. Pin in place.

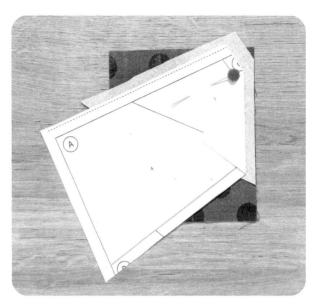

Tip: Right Sides Together   *As you are piecing, the right sides of the fabric should always be together.*

5 Flip the pattern flat and sew ¼" beyond the seamline at the beginning and the end of this seam, (as shown by the green line). No back tacking is needed, as the ends of the seams are stitched over by other seams. Notice that the fabric for Piece 2 is much larger than needed; it will be trimmed later.

Tip: Double-Check to Avoid Seam Ripping

I like to use large scraps (but no larger than 9″ × 11″) and then trim the piece after sewing it in place. As you place the fabric under your presser foot to sew, the seam allowance and the shape you are filling should be to your right. The shape you previously completed should be to your left. Before sewing, do a mental check. Ask yourself these two questions: "Is the piece I am working on to my right?" and "Is the majority of my fabric to my left?". If the answer is yes, then sew. This simple check will eliminate much seam ripping.

6 Flip the fabric into position behind Piece 2 and press. Pin in place to keep it flat.

7 Trim the fabric a generous ½" beyond the first edge of Piece 2 (see dotted lines). *Do not cut the pattern.*

8 Trim the fabric a generous ½" beyond the second edge of Piece 2.

9 Continue to add the remaining pieces in the same manner as you added Piece 2.

Segment A completed

Stitches Interfering?

Overstitching the seams may at times interfere with an exact fold along a stitching line. In this case, tear the paper just enough to release it from the stitching.

10 Trim the seam allowance of Segment A to an *exact ¼"* seam using a rotary cutter, a mat, and a ruler with a ¼" line. The segment is now ready to be sewn to the other segments. Follow the same process to make Segments B, C, D, and E.

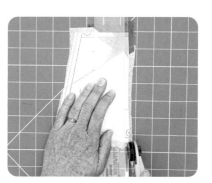

Joining Segments

Note: Make sure each segment is trimmed so that it has an exact ¼" seam allowance along the red segment seamline only. Do not trim the outer edge seam allowances at this time.

Segments have ¼" seam allowances where they will be joined.

1. With the right sides together, pin together the edges of Segments A and B, matching the red sewing lines. Push a straight pin through the end of each red line to help align them as closely as possible. Sew on the red line and ¼" past the red line on both ends.

Sew together segments on red line

2. Remove the paper from the seam allowance to eliminate the possibility of the paper getting trapped under the seams.

3. Press the seam to one side. Let the seam "show" you in which direction it wants to be pressed.

4. Continue joining segments until Hedgehog, Part 1, is complete. Repeat the process of paper-piecing, beginning with Preparing the Patterns (page 8) for Hedgehog, Part 2.

Joining Blocks

Blue lines show where to join the completed blocks. Unlike red segment seams, blue-line seams are backtacked at the beginning and end.

1. Trim only the edges on Part 1 and Part 2 that have a *blue* line. Trim these edges ¼" away from the blue line.

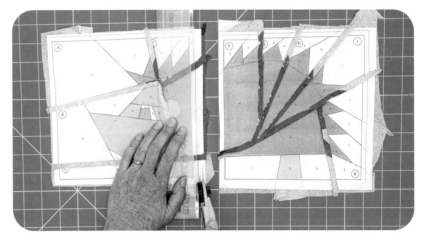

2. Pin the Part 1 and the Part 2 block, with right sides together, matching the blue lines.

3. Sew on the blue line, backtacking at the beginning and end of the seam. Rip the paper from the seam area. Press the block open.

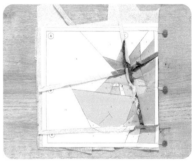

Finish Before Trimming

Make sure never to trim the excess fabric from the outer edges of the block until the block is finished and joined to its partner block. After that, it is safe to square up the block using a cutting mat, ruler, and rotary cutter. A rectangular block should measure 8" × 15½", unfinished.

4. Complete any embroidery *while* the paper is still attached. The paper acts as a stabilizer and will keep the block from stretching. *After* the block has been attached to the project, the paper may be removed.

Create seven fabulous home decor projects using any of the seventeen paper pieced blocks.

Lap Quilt

FINISHED SIZE: 46½″ × 56″

Materials

Fabric A: ¼ yard for inner border

Fabrics B, C, D, and E: ⅜ yard *each* for pieced blocks and pieced middle border

Fabric F: ½ yard for middle border (I used more of fabric B.)

Fabric G: 1½ yards for outer border and binding (I used more of fabric C.)

Fabric H: 3 yards for backing

Fabric I: ¾ yard background fabric for paper pieced blocks

Assorted scraps: For paper piecing blocks. (*See your selected block's materials list.*)

Batting: 1 rectangle 52″ × 62″

Black embroidery floss

Cutting

Yardages are based on 42″ usable width of fabric (WOF). Fold fabric selvage to selvage.

Fabric A

• Cut 4 strips 1½″ × WOF.

Fabric B, C, D, and E

• From *each* fabric cut 4 strips 2½″ × WOF.

Fabric F

• Cut 2 rectangles 7½″ × 25″ for middle border.

Fabric G

• Cut 5 strips 5½″ × WOF for outer border.

• Cut 6 strips 2½″ × WOF for binding.

Fabric H

• Cut 3 yards in half into 2 pieces each 1½ yards long.

Sewing

Use ¼″ seams throughout unless otherwise directed.

PAPER PIECED BLOCKS

Refer to Paper Piecing Basics (page 7) as needed.

1 Paper piece 6 selected square blocks, using Fabric I as the background fabric of each block and the assorted scraps for the rest of the block.

2 Add any necessary embroidery.

3 Trim each block to 8″ × 8″.

ASSEMBLE THE STRIPED BLOCKS

1 Sew each Fabric B 2½″ × WOF strip to a Fabric C 2½″ × WOF strip. Press the seams toward Fabric B.

2 Sew each Fabric D 2½″ × WOF strip to a Fabric E 2½″ × WOF strip. Press the seams toward Fabric D.

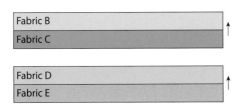

Sew 2 strips together of each of the 4 fabrics.

3 Sew the B/C strip to the D/E strips along the WOF edge. Press the seams in the same direction as the other seams.

4 Use 2 of the B/C/D/E strips to cut into 8″ segments. Trim 6 of these segments into 8″ × 8″ blocks. Save the 2 remaining B/C/D/E strips for the striped middle border.

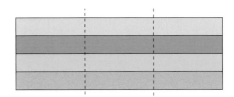

Sew 4 strips together and cut into blocks.

ASSEMBLE THE CENTER OF THE QUILT

1 Rows 1 and 3: Sew a paper pieced block to each side of a B/C/D/E block.

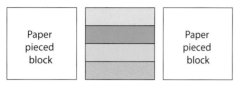

Rows 1 and 3

2 Rows 2 and 4: Sew a B/C/D/E block to each side of a paper pieced block.

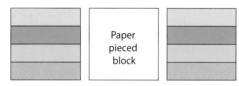

Rows 2 and 4

3 Sew rows 1 through 4 together.

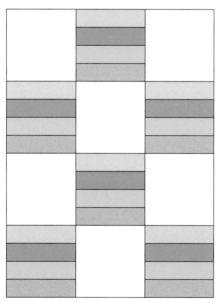

Assemble 4 rows

ATTACH THE INNER BORDER

1 Row 1: Sew a Fabric A 1½″ strip to the sides of the quilt. Press the seams toward the border. Trim the excess fabric.

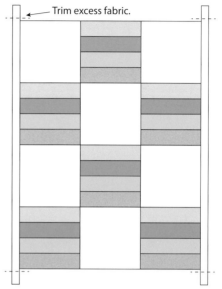

Attach inner border strip to sides of quilt

2 Sew a Fabric A 1½″ border to the top and bottom of the quilt. Press the seams toward the border. Trim the excess fabric.

3 Sew a Fabric F 7½″ × 25″ rectangle to the top and bottom of the quilt. Press the seams toward the inner border.

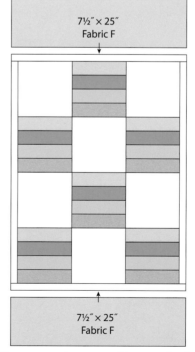

Sew a rectangle to top and bottom of quilt

ASSEMBLE THE STRIPED MIDDLE BORDER

1 Cut the remaining 2 B/C/D/E units into 6½″ wide blocks. Sew 6 of the 6½″ units together, with the stripes going horizontally. Press the seams in the same direction as the other seams. Repeat with the remaining 6 units, to make 2 striped border columns.

Sew 6 blocks of stripes together for 1 border.

2 Sew a striped border to each side of the quilt. Press the seams toward the sashing. Trim the excess fabric.

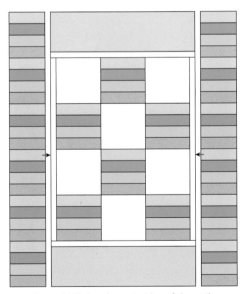

Sew middle border to 2 sides of the quilt

ATTACH THE OUTER BORDER

1 Sew a Fabric G 5½″ × WOF strip to the top and bottom of the quilt. Press the seams toward the border. Trim the excess fabric.

2 Cut 1 Fabric G 5½″ × WOF strip in half to create 2 rectangles 5½″ × 21″. Sew one of these short strips to each of the remaining 2 Fabric G strips to create 2 extra-long border strips. Press the seams to one side.

3 Sew these 2 extra-long strips to the sides of the quilt. Press the seams toward the border. Trim the excess fabric.

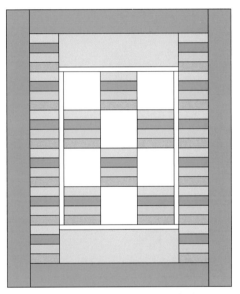

Quilt with outer borders attached

BACKING

Sew together the 2 Fabric H pieces selvage to selvage with a ¾″ seam allowance. Trim off the selvages in the seam allowance. Press open.

QUILTING

1 Remove the paper from the back of the blocks.

2 Layer the Fabric H prepared backing (right side facing down), batting, and quilt top (right side facing up).

3 Pin all 3 layers together and quilt as desired.

BINDING

1 Place two Fabric G 2½″ × WOF binding strips overlapping at a right angle, with right sides together. Mark a diagonal line from Corner A to Corner B. Sew on the diagonal line to connect the strips.

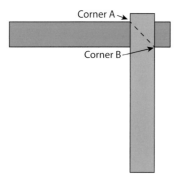

Strips overlap at a right angle. Mark diagonal line.

2 Trim the seam allowance to ¼″ and press to one side. Repeat to add the remaining four Fabric G 2½″ × WOF binding strips.

3 Press the binding strip in half lengthwise with the wrong sides together.

4 Beginning at the center of one side, align the raw edges of the binding strip with the raw edges of the quilt. Fold the beginning of the strip on a 90-degree angle (right angle) with the tail facing away from the quilt.

5 Stitch ¼″ from the raw edges. Stop stitching ¼″ from the first corner and back tack.

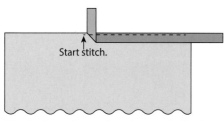

Pin binding strip to quilt and start stitching here

6 Fold the binding strip straight up. The raw edge of the binding strip should align with the raw edge of the second side of the quilt.

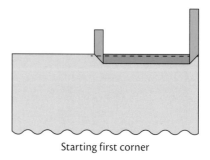

Starting first corner

7 Fold the binding strip straight down to overlap the second edge of the quilt, aligning the fold with the first side of the quilt. Start stitching at the top corner and continue until ¼″ from the next corner and back tack.

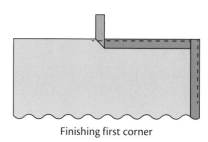

Finishing first corner

8 Continue in this manner around the remaining sides of the quilt, back tacking and turning at each corner.

9 Trim the end of the binding strip so it overlaps the angled beginning section by 2″. Trim away the remaining tail.

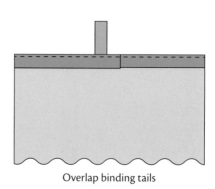

Overlap binding tails

10 Press the binding around to the back of the quilt and hand stitch in place, easing in the fullness where the tails overlap.

Baby Quilt

FINISHED SIZE: 36½″ × 30″

Materials

Fabric A: 1¼ yards for main fabric and background for paper pieced blocks

Fabric B: ⅜ yards for binding

Fabric C: 1 yard for backing

Assorted scraps: For paper piecing blocks. (*See your selected block's materials list.*)

Batting: 1 rectangle 36″ × 42″

Paper-backed fusible adhesive, 17″ wide: ⅜ yard (I use Heat*n*Bond Lite.)

Cutting

Yardages are based on 42″ usable width of fabric (WOF). Fold fabric selvage to selvage.

Fabric A

Cut these pieces before paper piecing

• Cut 1 rectangle 21″ × 30½″.

• Cut 1 rectangle 8½″ × 30½″.

Fabric B

• Cut 4 strips 2½″ × WOF for binding.

Fabric C

• Cut 1 rectangle 36″ × 42″ for backing.

Sewing

Use ¼″ seams throughout unless otherwise directed.

PAPER PIECED BLOCKS

Refer to Paper Piecing Basics (page 7) as needed.

1 Paper piece 2 selected rectangle blocks, using Fabric A as the background fabric of each block and the assorted scraps for the rest of the block.

Tip

Paper piece 1 right-facing koala block, and 1 left-facing koala block.

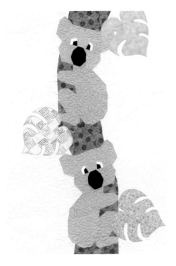

2 Add any necessary embroidery.

3 Trim each block to 8″ × 15½″.

4 Place the right-facing koala at the bottom. Sew the 2 finished koala blocks together to make a column. Press the seam allowance to one side.

Paper pieced block

Paper pieced block

Column of koalas

ASSEMBLE THE QUILT TOP

Sew a Fabric A 8½″ × 30½″ rectangle to the left side edge of the koala column. Press the seams away from the blocks. Sew a Fabric A 21″ × 30½″ rectangle to the right side edge of the koala column. Press the seams away from the blocks.

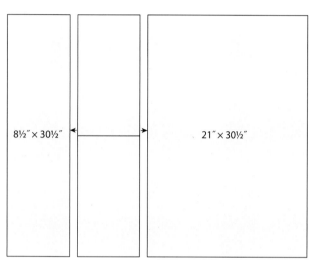

Sew rectangles to koala column

ATTACH THE APPLIQUED LEAVES

Using the paper-backed fusible adhesive, follow the manufacturer's directions to apply 3 leaves (page 21) to the quilt top. Refer to the photo of the finished quilt below for placement.

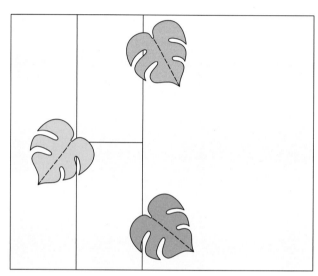

Leaf placement

QUILTING

1 Remove the paper from the back of the blocks.

2 Layer the Fabric C backing (right side facing down), batting, and quilt top (right side facing up).

3 Pin all 3 layers together. Satin stitch around the 3 leaves, going through all layers of the quilt. Quilt as desired. It is not necessary to quilt over the leaves.

BINDING

Follow the instructions in Lap Quilt, Binding (page 16), using the 4 Fabric B 2½″ × WOF strips.

Baby Quilt
Leaf
Make 3.

Oversized
Floor Pillow

FINISHED SIZE: 36″ × 36″

Materials

Fabric A: ¼ yard for paper pieced block borders

Fabric B: 1¾ yards for sashing, scallop piecing, outer border, and backing

Fabrics C and D: ¼ yard of each fabric for scallops

Fabric E: ⅜ yard for binding

Fabric F: 1 yard background fabric for paper pieced blocks

Assorted scraps: For paper piecing blocks. (*See your selected block's materials list.*)

Muslin: 1 square 40″ × 40″

Batting: 1 square 40″ × 40″

Zipper: 30″ long

Cotton web strapping: 12″ long

Pillow form: 36″ × 36″, or 3 pounds of fiberfill

Cutting

Yardages are based on 42″ usable width of fabric (WOF). Fold fabric selvage to selvage.

Fabric A

- Cut 6 strips 1″ × WOF. Subcut 8 strips 1″ × 16½″ and 8 strips 1″ × 8″.

Fabric B

For Sashing

- Cut 2 strips 1½″ × WOF. Subcut 1 strip 1½″ × 18½″ and 2 strips 1½″ × 16½″.

- Cut 3 strips 2″ × WOF. Subcut into 2 strips 2″ × 36½″ and 2 strips 2″ × 18½″.

For Scallop Piecing

- Cut 1 strip 2½″ × WOF. Subcut into 16 squares 2½″ × 2½″.

For Outer Border

- Cut 2 strips 4″ × WOF. Subcut into 2 strips 4″ × 36½″.

For Backing

- Cut 1 piece 36½″ × WOF.

Fabric C and D

- From *each* fabric cut 1 strip 4½″ × WOF. Subcut into 4 rectangles 4½″ × 9½″. There will be 8 total rectangles, 4 from Fabric C and 4 from Fabric D.

Fabric E

- Cut 4 strips 2½″ × WOF for binding.

Sewing

Use ¼″ seams throughout unless otherwise directed.

PAPER PIECED BLOCKS

① Paper piece 4 selected rectangle blocks, using Fabric F as the background fabric of each block and the assorted scraps for the rest of the block. All 4 rectangle blocks must be oriented in the same direction.

② Add any necessary embroidery.

③ Trim each block to 8″ × 15½″.

ATTACH THE PAPER PIECED BLOCK BORDERS

① Sew a Fabric A 1″ × 8″ border to the top and bottom of each rectangular block. Press the seams toward the border.

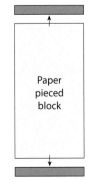

Paper pieced block

Sew border to top and bottom of blocks

2 Sew a Fabric A 1″ × 16½″ border to the sides of each block. Press the seams toward the border.

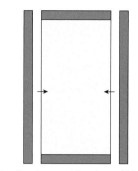

Sew borders to side edges of blocks

ATTACH THE SASHING TO THE BLOCKS

1 Sew a Fabric B 1½″ × 16½″ sashing strip to connect 2 rectangular blocks, side by side. Repeat with the remaining two blocks. Press the seams toward the sashing.

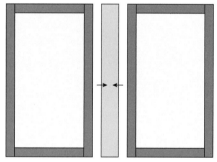

Connect 2 blocks with sashing.

2 Sew a Fabric B 1½″ × 18½″ sashing strip to connect the top set of blocks to the bottom set of blocks. Press the seams toward the sashing.

3 Sew a Fabric B 2″ × 18½″ strip to the top and bottom of the block unit. Press the seams toward the sashing.

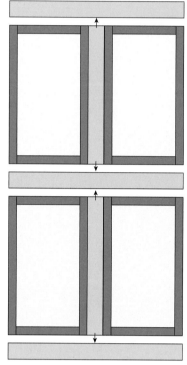

Sew sashing to top, middle, and bottom of block units.

4 Sew a Fabric B 2″ × 36½″ sashing strip to each side of the unit. Press the seams toward the sashing.

Sew sashing to sides

ASSEMBLE THE SCALLOPS

1 Pin a Fabric B 2½″ × 2½″ square in the top corners of a Fabric C 4½″ × 9½″ rectangle, right sides together. Draw a diagonal line from corner to corner on the back of each square. Sew on the diagonal line in each square.

Sew squares to top corners

2 Trim excess fabric ¼″ from each diagonal line Press the seam allowance toward the outer corners.

Finished scallop

3 Repeat Step 1 and 2 with every Fabric C and D 4½″ × 9½″ rectangle.

4 Alternating colors, sew 4 units together to make 2 borders for the sides of the pillow. Sew the 2 borders to the sides of the pillow. Press the seams toward the sashing.

Four scallops make one border

ATTACH THE OUTER BORDERS

1 Sew a Fabric B 4″ × 36½″ border to the 2 sides edges of the pillow, next to the scallops. Press the seam allowance to the borders.

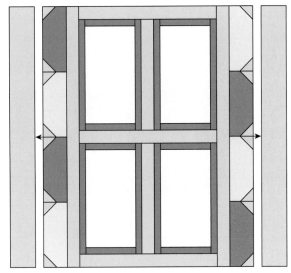

Outer border on 2 side edges

PREPARE THE PILLOW BACK

1 With the Fabric B 36½″ piece of backing folded selvage to selvage, trim away the selvages and trim ½″ from the folded edge. This will create 2 pieces approximately 20″ wide × 36½″ long.

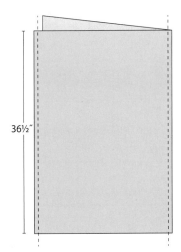

36½″

Trim both edges of pillow backing

2 Place the 2 rectangle pieces right sides together. On a 36½″ edge, make a mark 3¼″ from the top and 3¼″ from the bottom.

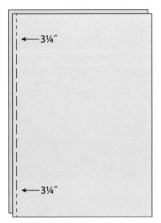

←— 3¼″

←— 3¼″

Markings at top and bottom

3 Using a ⅝″ seam allowance, sew using a regular stitch length from the top to the first marking, and back tack at the 3¼″ marking. Change the stitch length to a basting stitch, and continue to sew to the second 3¼″ marking. Change the stitch length back to regular stitch length, back-tack, and sew to the end. Press the seam open.

ADD THE ZIPPER

1 Pin the 30″ zipper to the back of the seam that was just pressed open. The front of the zipper should be facing the seam, directly behind the basted portion of the seam. Pin in place.

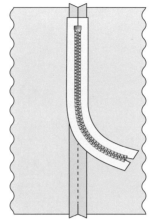

Pin zipper to back of seam

2 Use a zipper foot to sew the zipper tape to the pillow backing. Pull the zipper tab down and out of the way, then back again after sewing the top portion of the zipper tape. Continue to sew around the zipper tape.

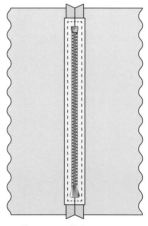

Sew around zipper tape

3 Use a seam ripper to open the basted stitches from the right side of the pillow backing. Remove the tiny threads. The pillow backing will measure 36½″ wide but will be longer than needed. Do not trim at this time.

Tip

A lint brush works well to remove the tiny threads.

QUILT

1 Remove the paper from the back of the paper pieced blocks.

2 Pin the front of the pillow right side facing up, the batting, and the muslin together.

3 Quilt as desired.

4 Trim the front of the pillow to 36½″ × 36½″.

ASSEMBLE AND BIND THE PILLOW

1 With *wrong* sides together, pin the front of the pillow to the pillow backing, orienting the pillow zipper horizontally. The pillow backing will be longer than the pillow front. Trim the pillow backing to match the pillow front.

2 Center the 12″ piece of cotton strapping on the right side of the pillow back. The distance between the outside edges of the strap ends should measure 6½″. Pin in place.

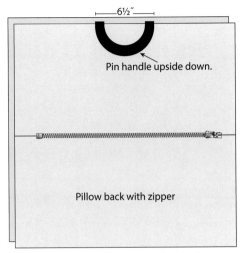

Pin handle upside down to pillow backing

BINDING

Follow the instructions in Lap Quilt, Binding (page 16). Start the binding at the bottom of the pillow. Binding will be sewn over the cotton strapping handle ends.

FILL THE PILLOW

Insert the pillow form or fill the pillow with the fiberfill.

Pillowcase with Flap

FINISHED SIZE: 17½˝ × 28˝

Materials

Fabric A: 1 yard for main fabric

Fabric B: ⅛ yard for accent strips

Fabric C: ⅜ yard for cuff

Fabric D: ⅓ yard background fabric for paper pieced block

Assorted scraps: For paper piecing blocks and appliqué letters (See your selected block's materials list).

Muslin: ¾ yard for backing of quilted front.

Batting: 1 rectangle 21″ × 25″

Paper-backed fusible adhesive, 17″ wide: ¼ yard (I use HeatnBond Lite.)

Cutting

Yardages are based on 42″ usable width of fabric (WOF). Fold fabric selvage to selvage.

Fabric A

• Cut 1 rectangle 19″ × 36″ for pillowcase back.

• Cut 2 rectangles 3¼″ × 23″ for pillowcase front.

Fabric B

• Cut 2 strips 1½″ × 23″ for accent strips.

Fabric C

• Cut 1 rectangle 12½″ × 19″ for cuff.

Fabric D

Cut these pieces before paper piecing

• Cut 1 rectangle 4″ × 23″.

• Cut 2 rectangles 4¼″ × 8″.

Muslin

• Cut 1 rectangle 21″ × 25″.

Sewing

Use ¼″ seams throughout unless otherwise directed.

PAPER PIECED BLOCK

Refer to Paper Piecing Basics (page 7) as needed.

1 Paper piece 1 selected horizontal rectangular block, using Fabric D as the background fabric and the assorted scraps for the rest of the block.

2 Add any necessary embroidery.

3 Trim the rectangular block to 8″ × 15½″.

CONSTRUCT THE PILLOWCASE FRONT

1 Sew a Fabric D 4¼″ × 8″ rectangle to each side of the rectangular block. Press the seams toward Fabric D.

2 Sew the Fabric D 4″ × 23″ rectangle to the top of the block unit. Press the seams toward Fabric D.

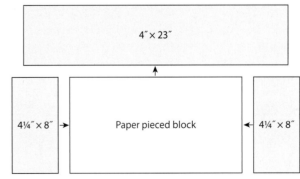

Sew pieces to paper-pieced block

3 Sew a Fabric B 1½″ × 23″ strip to the top and bottom of the block unit. Press the seams toward the strip.

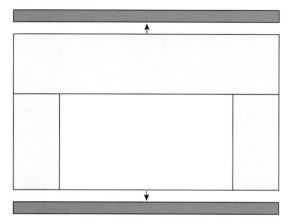

Sew strips to top and bottom

4 Sew a Fabric A 3¼″ × 23″ rectangle to the top and bottom of the paper pieced unit. Press the seams toward the Fabric B strip.

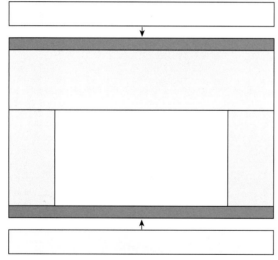

Sew rectangles to top and bottom

APPLIQUE LETTERS AND QUILT

1 Remove the paper from the back of the block.

2 Layer the muslin rectangle, batting, and pillow top (right side facing up).

3 Pin all 3 layers together. Avoid pinning the center area of the 4″ rectangle above the paper pieced block, as this area is for the appliqué letters.

4 Following the manufacturer's directions, cut out fabric letters using the *Ultra Bond Lite* and the reversed alphabet letters (pages 33–35). Arrange the letters in the 4″ rectangle area above the paper pieced block. Satin stitch around the letters, stitching through all layers.

5 Quilt the pillowcase top as desired.

6 Trim the pillowcase top to 19″ × 23″.

ATTACH THE CUFF

1 Pin the Fabric C 12½″ × 23″ cuff under the pillow front, with the right side of the cuff facing the wrong side of the pillow.

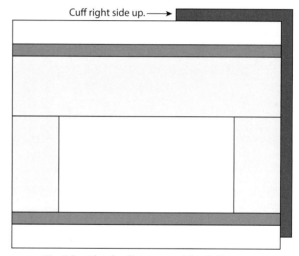

Cuff right side up. ⟶

Pin right side of cuff to wrong side of pillowcase.

2 Roll the pillowcase front into a tight tube that will fit in the center of the cuff.

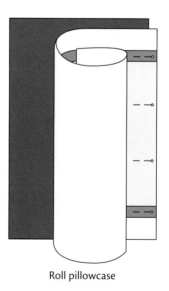

Roll pillowcase

3 Wrap the cuff around the rolled-up pillowcase, and pin over the already pinned edge.

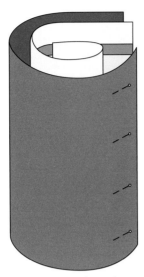

3 layers pinned together

4 Sew the pinned edge of the pillowcase and cuff, sewing through all layers. Reach inside the tube and pull the pillowcase out through one side of the tube. Flatten the cuff and press. All raw edges are encased inside the cuff.

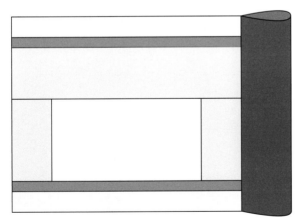

Pull pillowcase out of the cuff tube

PREPARE THE PILLOWCASE BACK

1 Press ¼" on one 23" side edge of the Fabric A 19" × 36" pillowcase back. Press another ¼" on the same edge and stitch this skinny hem in place.

2 Place the pillowcase back behind the pillow front, wrong sides together.

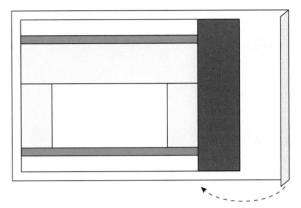

Pillowcase front and back, wrong sides together

ASSEMBLE THE PILLOWCASE

1 Fold the hemmed edge of the pillowcase back over the cuff and press. The hemmed edge should extend about 7" over the pillowcase top to form the "flap".

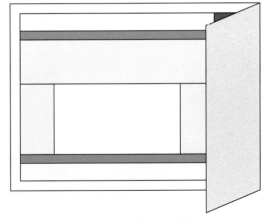

Press hemmed edge to a 7" flap.

2 Slide the 7″ flap under the pillowcase front cuff, and pin in place. Stitch the 3 sides of the pillowcase together, leaving the cuffed edge open. Stitching the wrong sides together starts to create a French seam.

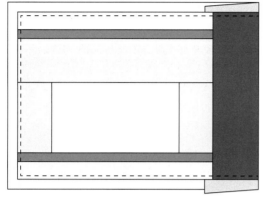

Stitch pillowcase front to pillowcase back.

3 Trim the seams to ⅛″. Turn the pillowcase wrong side out and poke the corners square. Pull the flap out and around to the outside of the pillowcase and press the 3 stitched sides. Pin the 3 stitched edges.

4 Stitch around the 3 previously stitched edges again, using a generous ¼″ seam allowance. This will encase the ⅛″ seam and create the French seam. No exposed seams!

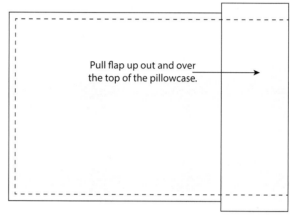

Pull flap up out and over the top of the pillowcase.

Stitch generous ¼″ seam.

5 Turn the finished pillowcase right sides out, and press. Too cute!

Table Runner

FINISHED SIZE: 11½″ × 42″

Materials

Fabric A: ½ yard for main fabric

Fabric B: ⅓ yard for binding

Fabric C: 1½ yards for backing

Fabric D: ¾ yard for background fabric for paper pieced blocks

Assorted scraps: For paper piecing blocks (*See your selected block's materials list.*)

Batting: 1 rectangle 18″ × 48″

Cutting

Yardages are based on 42″ usable width of fabric (WOF). Fold fabric selvage to selvage.

Fabric A

- Cut 1 strip 4½″ × WOF. Subcut into 4 rectangles 4½″ × 8″.

- Cut 1 square 9″ × 9″. Subcut in half on the diagonal to form 2 triangles.

Fabric B

- Cut 3 strips 2½″ × WOF for binding.

Fabric C

- Cut 1 rectangle 18″ × 48″ for backing.

Sewing

Use ¼″ seams throughout unless otherwise directed.

PAPER PIECED BLOCKS

Refer to Paper Piecing Basics (page 7) as needed.

1 Paper piece 4 selected square blocks, using Fabric D as the background fabric of each block and the assorted scraps for the rest of the block.

2 Add any necessary embroidery.

3 Trim each block to 8″ × 8″.

ASSEMBLE THE BLOCKS

1 Sew a Fabric A 4½″ × 8″ rectangle to the top of 2 blocks, and to the bottom of the remaining 2 blocks. Press the seams toward the main fabric.

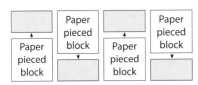

Sew a rectangle to top or bottom of each block.

2 Sew the 4 block units together. Press the seams open.

Sew block units together

3 Sew the widest side of a Fabric A triangle to each end of the block unit. Press the seams toward the triangles.

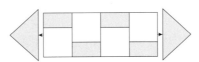

Add triangles on each end.

QUILTING

1 Remove the paper from the back of the blocks.

2 Layer the Fabric C backing (right side facing down), batting, and table runner top (right side facing up).

3 Pin all 3 layers together and quilt as desired.

4 Trim backing and batting even with triangles and edges.

BINDING

Follow the instructions in Lap Quilt, Binding (page 16), using the 3 Fabric B 2½″ × WOF strips.

Wall Hanging

FINISHED SIZE: 19½″ × 23″

Materials

Fabric A: ⅓ yard for sashing

Fabric B: 1 yard for backing, and hanging sleeve

Fabric C: ⅓ yard for binding

Fabric D: ¾ yard background fabric for paper pieced blocks

Assorted scraps: For paper piecing blocks (*See your selected block's materials list.*)

Batting: 1 rectangle 25″ × 33″

Cutting

Yardages are based on 42″ usable width of fabric (WOF). Fold fabric selvage to selvage.

Fabric A

• Cut 4 strips 2″ × WOF. Subcut into: 3 rectangles 2″ × 24½″, 2 rectangles 2″ × 20″, 3 rectangles 2″ × 8″.

Fabric B

• Cut 1 rectangle 25″ × 33″ for backing.

• Cut 1 rectangle 8½″ × 25″ for hanging sleeve.

Fabric C

• Cut 3 strips 2½″ × WOF for binding.

Sewing

Use ¼″ seams throughout unless otherwise directed.

PAPER PIECED BLOCKS

Refer to Paper Piecing Basics (page 7) as needed.

1 Paper piece 3 selected square blocks, 1 selected horizontal rectangular block, and 1 Flower Block, (page 70) using Fabric D as the background fabric, and the assorted scraps for the rest of the blocks.

2 Add any necessary embroidery.

3 Trim each square block to 8″ × 8″. Trim the rectangular block to 8″ × 15½″. Trim the Flower Block to 6½″ wide × 8″ high. If not using the Flower Block, cut a Fabric D rectangle 6½″ × 8″ to substitute for the Flower Block.

ATTACH THE SASHING TO THE BLOCKS

1 Sew a Fabric A 2″ × 8″ strip to each side of the Flower Block (or the Fabric C 6″ × 8″ rectangle). Press the seams toward the sashing.

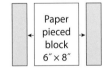

Sew a strip to each side of block

2 Sew a square block to each side of the unit created in Step 1. Press the seams toward the sashing. This unit will become Row 1.

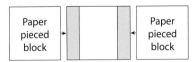

Sew a square block to each side.

3 Sew a Fabric A 2″ × 8″ strip to connect the rectangular block to the remaining square block. Press the seams toward the sashing. This unit will become Row 2.

Connect rectangular block to square block

4 Sew a Fabric A 2″ × 24½″ strip to the top and bottom of Row 1. Press the seams toward the sashing.

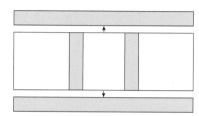
Sew sashing to top and bottom of Row 1

5 Sew a Fabric A 2″ × 24½″ strip to the bottom of Row 2. Press the seams toward the sashing.

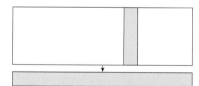
Sew sashing to bottom of Row 2

6 Sew Row 1 to Row 2. Press the seams toward the sashing.

7 Sew a Fabric A 2″ × 20″ strip to the 2 sides of the wall hanging. Press the seams toward the sashing.

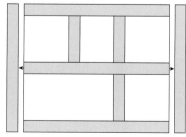
Sew Row 1 to Row 2.

QUILTING

1 Remove the paper from the back of the blocks.

2 Layer the Fabric B backing (right side facing down), batting, and wall hanging top (right side facing up).

3 Pin all 3 layers together and quilt as desired.

BINDING

Follow the instructions in Lap Quilt, Binding (page 16), using the 3 Fabric C 2½″ × WOF strips.

HANGING SLEEVE

1 Press under ¼″ on each 8½″ end of the Fabric B 8½″ × 25″ rectangle. Press under another ½″. Sew these hems in place close to the pressed edges.

2 With right sides together, sew together the long edges of Fabric B to form a tube. Turn the tube right side out and press it flat, centering the seam down the center back of the hanging tube.

3 On the back of the wall hanging, pin the tube to the top of the wall hanging directly beneath the binding. Hand stitch the sleeve in place all the way around, leaving the short ends of the tube open.

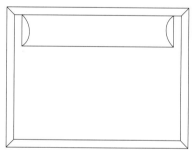
Hanging sleeve on back of wall hanging

Tote With Zipper

FINISHED SIZE: 15″ × 15″

Materials

Fabric A: ½ yard for main fabric

Fabric B: ⅓ yard for pocket lining

Fabric C: ½ yard for tote lining

Fabric D: ¼ yard background fabric for paper pieced block

Assorted scraps: For paper piecing blocks. (*See your selected block's materials list.*)

Fusible batting: 1 rectangle 8¾″ × 15½″

One-sided fusible stabilizer: 1 yard (such as Bosal In-R-Foam Single Sided Fusible Foam Stabilizer)

Heavy duty grommets, 12mm: 4

Cording, 8mm-wide: 2½ yards

Zipper: 16″

Cutting

Yardages are based on 42″ usable width of fabric (WOF). Fold fabric selvage to selvage.

Fabric A

• Cut 2 squares 15½″ × 15½″.

Fabric B

• Cut 1 rectangle 10¼″ × 15½″.

Fabric C

• Cut 2 squares 15½″ × 15½″.

Fusible stabilizer

• Cut 2 squares 15½″ × 15½″.

Sewing

Use ¼″ seams throughout unless otherwise directed.

PAPER PIECED BLOCK

Refer to Paper Piecing Basics (page 7) as needed.

1 Paper piece 1 selected horizontally oriented rectangle block, using Fabric D as the background fabric for the block and the assorted scraps for the rest of the block.

2 Add any necessary embroidery.

3 Trim the block to 8″ × 15½″.

4 Remove the paper from the back of the block.

ASSEMBLE THE OUTER POCKET

1 Right sides together, sew the Fabric B 10¼″ × 15½″ rectangle to the top of the paper pieced block. Press the seams toward the pocket lining.

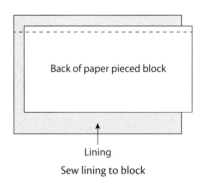

Back of paper pieced block

Lining

Sew lining to block

2 Steam press the fusible batting 8¾″ × 15½″ to the back of the paper pieced block. It will extend 1″ into the lining. Press the lining to the back of the block and pin it in place. Top stitch in the ditch where the block and the lining meet, and top stitch ¼″ from the top of the pocket lining. Quilt pocket as desired.

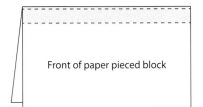

Topstitch at the top of the pocket and in the ditch.

PREPARE THE MAIN FABRIC

1 Using a damp pressing cloth, steam press the one-sided fusible stabilizer to the back of each Fabric A 15½″ × 15½″ square.

2 Pin the outer pocket at the bottom of one of the Fabric A 15½″ × 15½″ squares. This piece will be the front of the tote. Baste the side and bottom edges of the pocket to the main fabric.

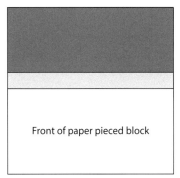

Pin pocket to main fabric piece and baste

ADDING THE ZIPPER

1 With right sides together, pin the zipper tape to the top of the tote front. The beginning of the tape should line up with the side edge of the tote, and the end of the tape will extend about 1″ beyond the opposite side edge. Using a zipper foot, sew the zipper tape to the top of the tote front section.

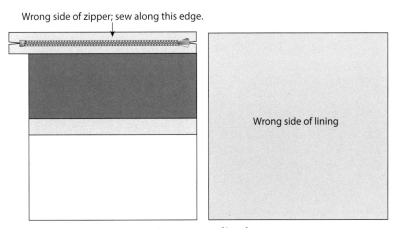

Sew zipper to top of bag front

2 Pin a Fabric C 15½″ × 15½″ lining square at the top of the tote, with the right side of the lining facing the wrong side of the zipper tape. Stitch over the previous stitching.

3 Press the lining to the back of the tote. The un-sewn edge of the zipper tape should now be exposed along the top of the tote.

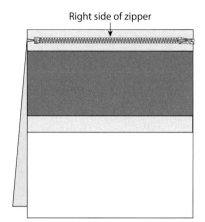

Front of bag with zipper at top, and lining in back

4 Repeat Steps 1–3 to add the back of the tote and its lining, to the opposite side of the zipper tape.

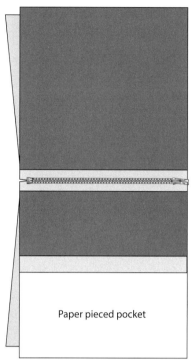

Paper pieced pocket

Main body of tote with lining pieces and zipper in place

SEW MAIN BODY AND LINING

1 Flip the 2 main body pieces with right sides together. Flip the 2 lining pieces with right sides together. Pin all the way around, leaving a 7″ turning hole on one edge of the lining. Match the top edges of the main body as cleanly as possible, folding the zipper lengthwise and squishing it to flatten.

2 Sew a generous ¼″ seam all the way around, back tacking before and after the 7″ turning hole. If using a nylon zipper, it may be possible to sew over the top of the zipper. Otherwise, stop stitching near the zipper, back tack, and start sewing on the other side.

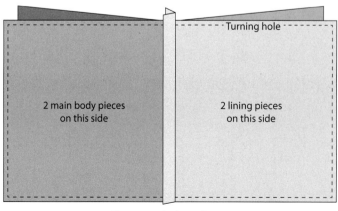

Sew around edges of tote

3 Clip the corners of the seams. Turn the tote right side out through the turning hole. Hand stitch the turning hole closed. Push the lining into the tote, securely into each bottom corner.

GROMMETS

1 Measure 1½" down from the top of the tote and 2½" from each side edge to mark the placement of each grommet.

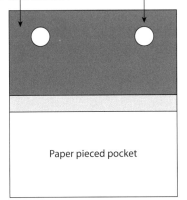

Grommet placement is 2½" from each side

Grommet placement is 1½" down from the top

Paper pieced pocket

Grommet placement

2 Attach the grommets following the manufacturer's directions.

3 Cut the 2½ yards of cording in half. Thread a piece of cording into each pair of grommets on a side, placing the knots on the inside of the tote.

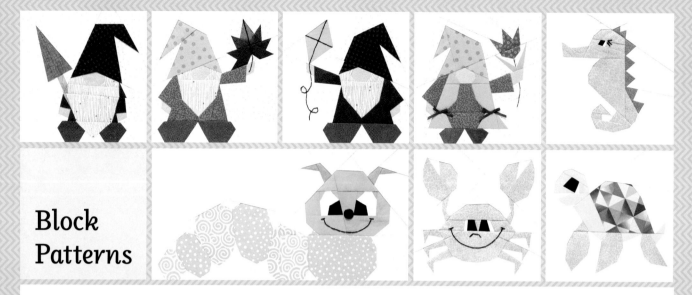

Block Patterns

- When making the blocks, refer to Paper-Piecing Basics (page 7) as needed.

- Refer to the specific project instructions about when to remove foundation papers.

- Any hand embroidery included in the following block instructions is meant to be done with foundation papers attached. (I use a running stitch or make French knots, with 6 strands of embroidery floss.)

- The first fabric in the materials list is for the block background. If your project includes background fabric in its materials list, you can ignore the background fabric listed for the block.

- *For baby's safety*: If you are making a quilt intended for a baby, for safety reasons, no buttons or other embellishments besides embroidery floss should be used. Be sure not to use any buttons or embellishments that could present a choking hazard.

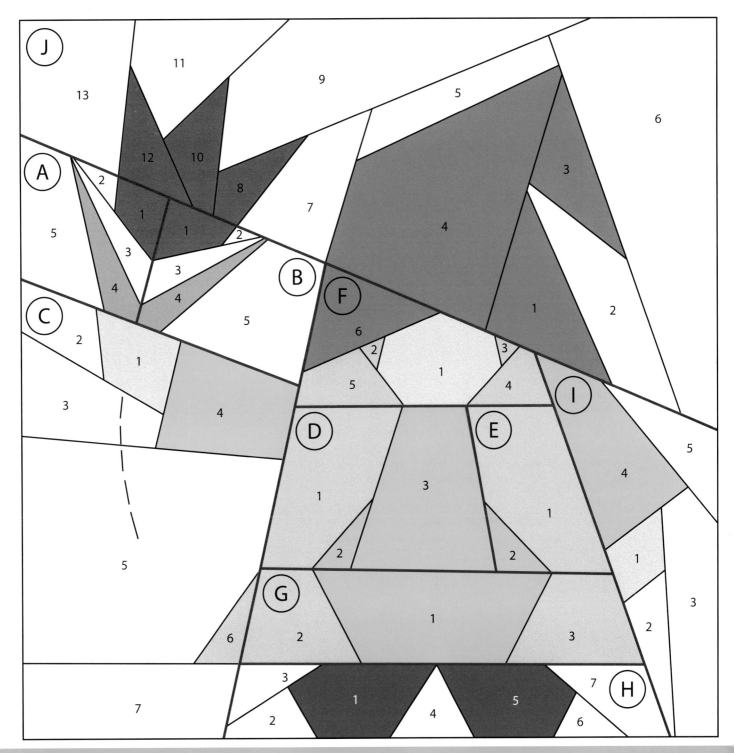

GNOME WITH FLOWER

Materials

- Large scrap of white, at least 9″ × 11″, for background
- Scraps of light green, dark green, peach, gold, brown, and pink
- Green embroidery floss
- Scraps of ⅛″ pink satin ribbon

Directions

For detailed directions, refer to Paper-Piecing Basics (page 7).

1. Make 4 copies of the pattern (A/F/G, B/E/H, C/J, D/I).

2. Cut around each segment, adding ¼″ seam allowances.

3. Paper piece each segment.

4. Connect the segments: A to B; A/B to C; D to E; D/E to F to G to H; D–H to I; A/B/C to F–I to J.

5. Trim the block to 8″ × 8″.

6. Hand stitch the stem with green embroidery floss.

7. Tie 2 tiny bows with ⅛″ satin ribbon. Hot glue or hand sew them to the pig tails. Refer to the photo of the block for placement.

Block Patterns   47

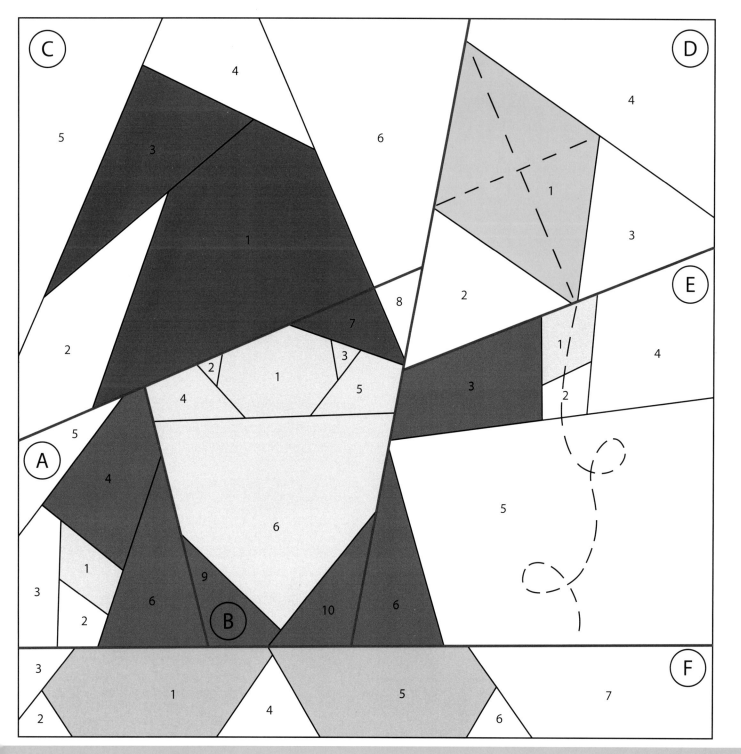

GNOME WITH KITE

Materials

- Large scrap of white, at least 9″ × 11″, for background
- Scraps of light red, dark red, peach, green, light gray, and medium gray
- Black embroidery floss

Directions

For detailed directions, refer to Paper-Piecing Basics (page 7).

1. Make 4 copies of the pattern (A/D, C/E, B, F).

2. Cut around each segment, adding ¼″ seam allowances.

3. Paper piece each segment.

4. Connect the segments: A to B; A/B to C; D to E; A/B/C to D/E to F.

5. Trim the block to 8″ × 8″.

6. Hand stitch the kite and kite tail using black embroidery floss.

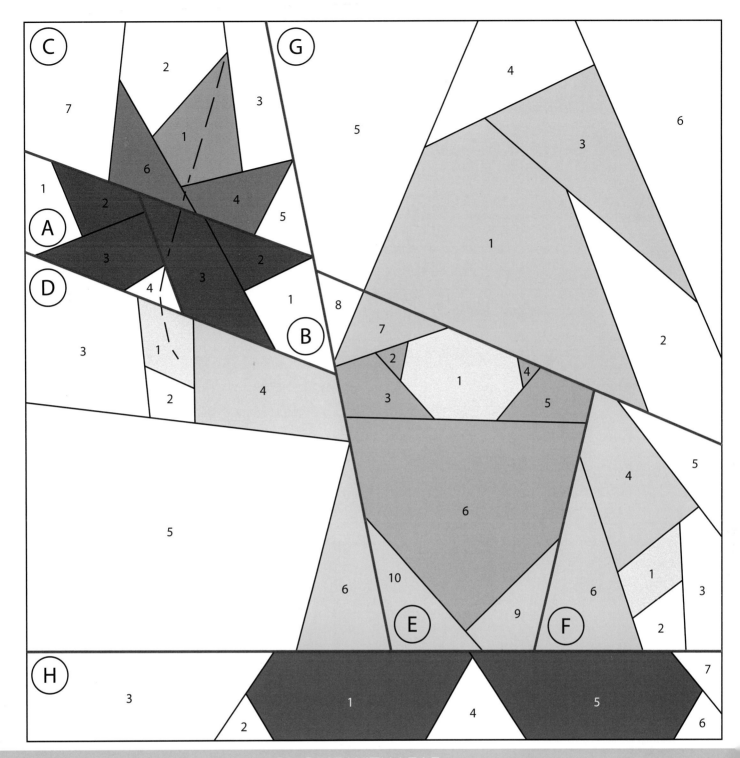

GNOME WITH LEAF

Materials

- Large scrap of white, at least 9″ × 11″, for background
- Scraps of light green, dark green, peach, brown, gray, orange, light red, and dark red
- Black embroidery floss

Directions

For detailed directions, refer to Paper-Piecing Basics (page 7).

1. Make 4 copies of the pattern (A/G/H, B/F, C/D, E).

2. Cut around each segment, adding ¼″ seam allowances.

3. Paper piece each segment.

4. Connect the segments: A to B; A/B to C to D; E to F; E/F to G; A–D to E/F/G to H.

5. Trim the block to 8″ × 8″.

6. Hand stitch the leaf vein and stem using black embroidery floss.

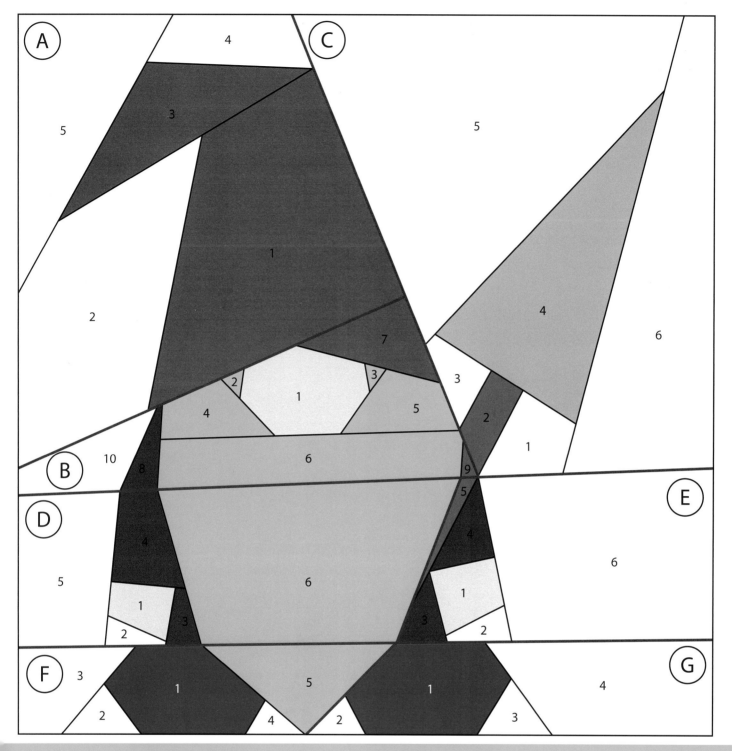

GNOME WITH TREE

Materials

- Large scrap of white, at least 9" × 11", for background
- Scraps of red, dark red, peach, black, gray, and green

Directions

For detailed directions, refer to Paper-Piecing Basics (page 7).

1. Make 4 copies of the pattern (A/D, B/G, C/F, E).

2. Cut around each segment, adding ¼" seam allowances.

3. Paper piece each segment.

4. Connect the segments: A to B; A/B to C; D to E; F to G; A/B/C to D/E to F/G.

5. Trim the block to 8" × 8".

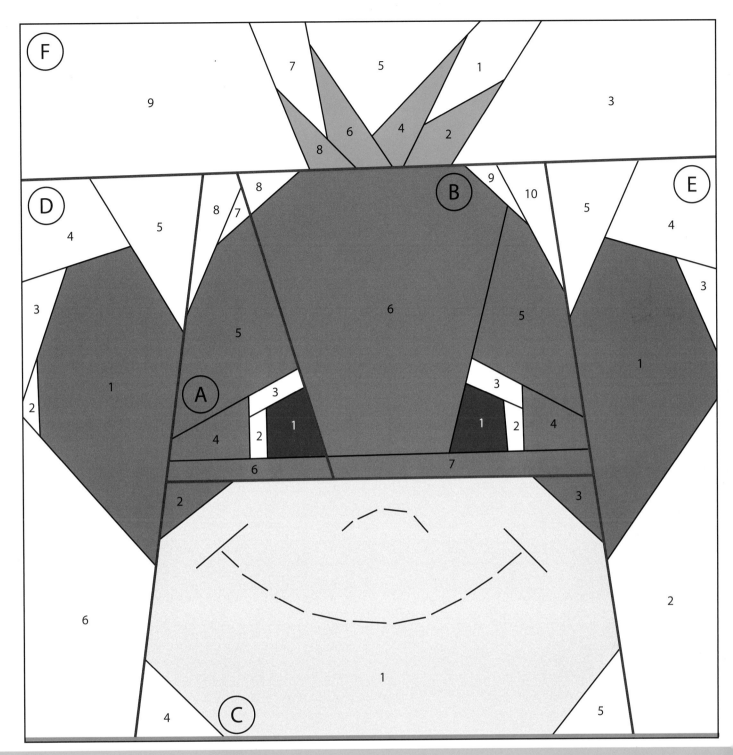

Materials

- Large scrap of white, at least 9″ × 11″, for background
- Scraps of brown, dark brown, tan, and black
- Black embroidery floss

Directions

For detailed directions, refer to Paper-Piecing Basics (page 7).

1. Make 3 copies of the pattern (A/E, B/D, C/F).
2. Cut around each segment, adding ¼″ seam allowances.
3. Paper piece each segment.
4. Connect the segments: A to B; A/B to C; A/B/C to D to E; A–E to F.
5. Trim ¼″ from the blue line.
6. Continue to Monkey, Part 2 (next page).

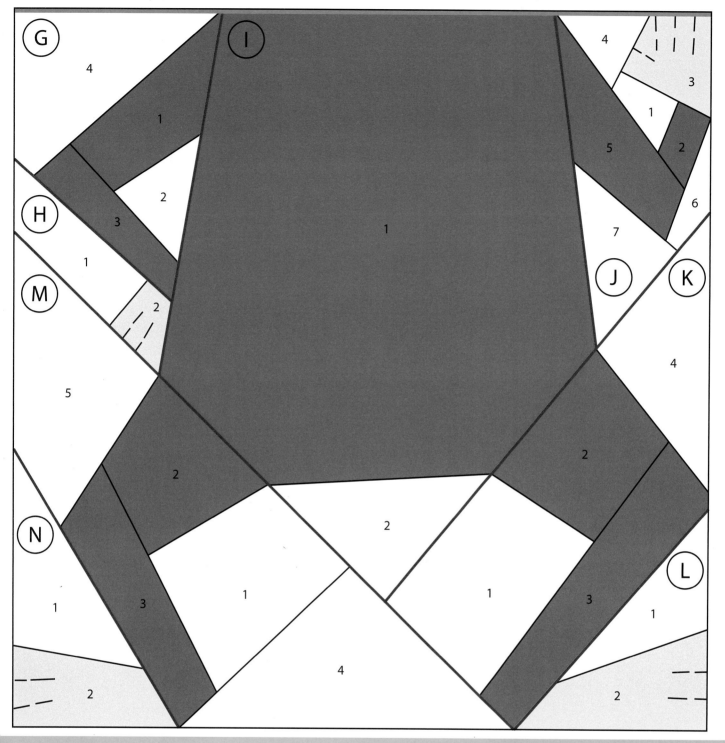

Materials

- Large scrap of white, at least 9″ × 11″, for background
- Scraps of brown, and tan
- Black embroidery floss

Directions

For detailed directions, refer to Paper-Piecing Basics (page 7).

1. Make 3 copies of the pattern (G/J/M, H/K, I/L/N).

2. Cut around each segment, adding ¼″ seam allowances.

3. Paper piece each segment.

4. Connect the segments: G to H; G/H to I to J; G–J to K to L; G–L to M to N.

5. Trim ¼″ from the blue line. Match and sew Part 1 to Part 2 on the blue lines.

6. Trim the block to 8″ × 15½″.

7. Hand stitch the nose, mouth, fingers, and toes using black embroidery floss.

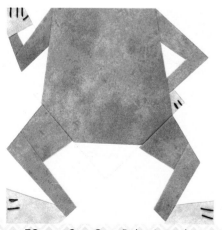

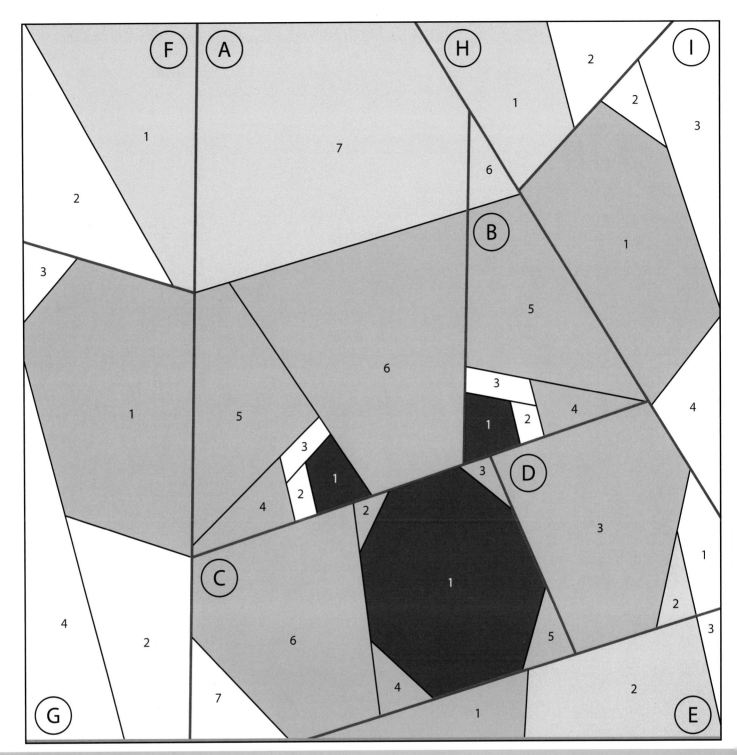

Materials

- Large scrap of light gray, at least 9″ × 11″, for background (pictured as white on the pattern)
- Scraps of brown, gray, black, and white

Directions

For detailed directions, refer to Paper-Piecing Basics (page 7).

1. Make 4 copies of the pattern (A/E/I, B/G, C/F, D/H).

2. Cut around each segment, adding ¼″ seam allowances.

3. Paper piece each segment.

4. Connect the segments: A to B; C to D; A/B to C/D to E; F to G; H to I; A–E to F/G to H/I.

5. Trim ¼″ from the blue line.

6. Continue to Koala, Part 2 (next page).

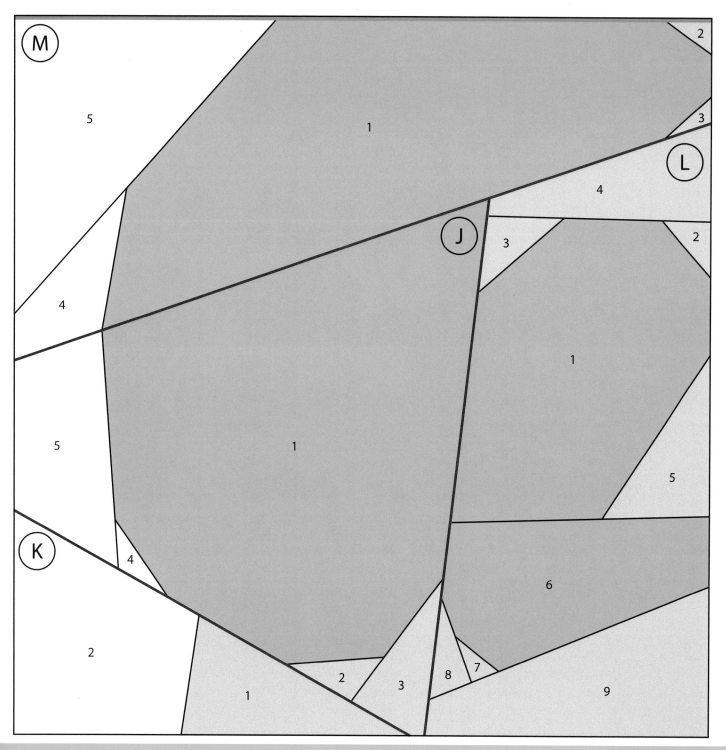

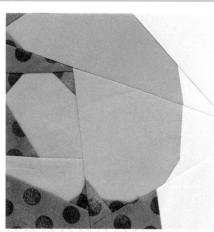

Materials

- Large scrap of light gray, at least 9″ × 11″, for background (pictured as white on the pattern)
- Scraps of brown, and gray

Directions

For detailed directions, refer to Paper-Piecing Basics (page 7).

1. Make 3 copies of the pattern (J, K/M, L).

2. Cut around each segment, adding ¼″ seam allowances.

3. Paper piece each segment.

4. Connect the segments: J to K; J/K to L; J/K/L to M.

5. Trim ¼″ from the blue line. Match and sew Part 1 to Part 2 on the blue lines.

6. Trim the block to 8″ × 15½″.

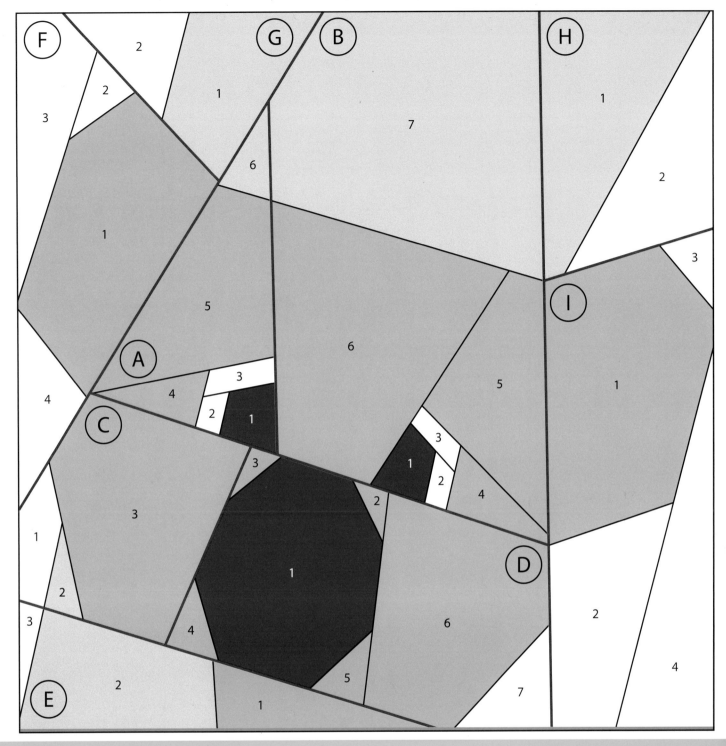

Materials

- Large scrap of light gray, at least 9″ × 11″, for background (pictured as white on the pattern)
- Scraps of brown, gray, black, and white

Directions

For detailed directions, refer to Paper-Piecing Basics (page 7).

1. Make 4 copies of the pattern (A/I, B/E/F, C/G, D/H).

2. Cut around each segment, adding ¼″ seam allowances.

3. Paper piece each segment.

4. Connect the segments: A to B; C to D; A/B to C/D to E; F to G; H to I; A–E to F/G to H/I.

5. Trim ¼″ from the blue line.

6. Continue to Koala Reversed, Part 2 (next page).

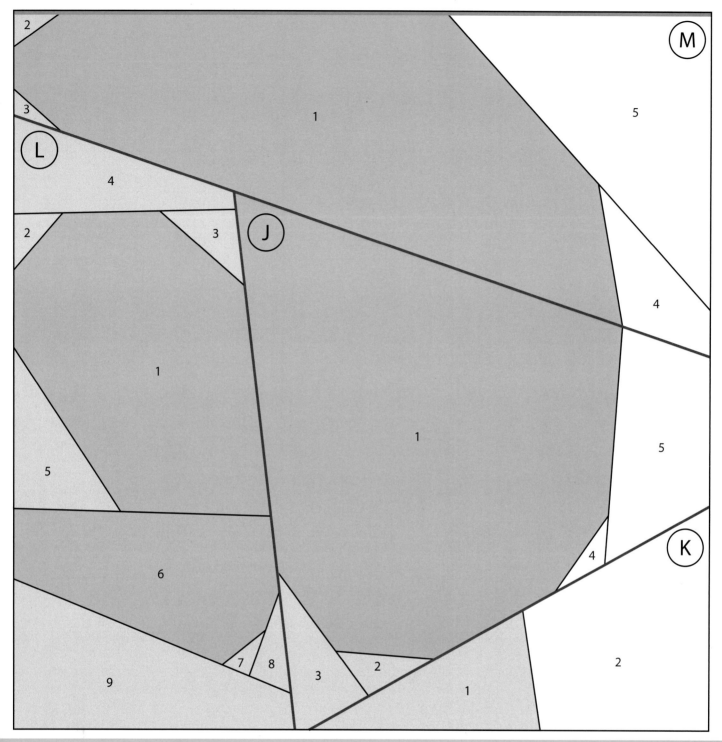

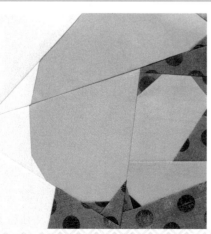

Materials

- Large scrap of light gray, at least 9″ × 11″, for background (pictured as white on the pattern)
- Scraps of brown, and gray

Directions

For detailed directions, refer to Paper-Piecing Basics (page 7).

1. Make 3 copies of the pattern (J, K/M, L).

2. Cut around each segment, adding ¼″ seam allowances.

3. Paper piece each segment.

4. Connect the segments: J to K; J/K to L; J/K/L to M.

5. Trim ¼″ from the blue line. Match and sew Part 1 to Part 2 on the blue lines.

6. Trim the block to 8″ × 15½″.

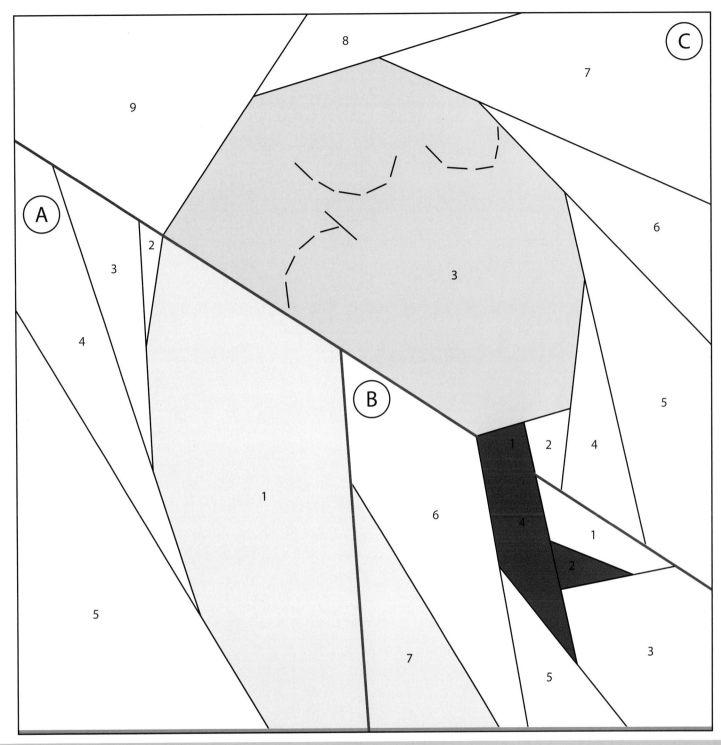

SNAKE, PART 1

Materials

- Large scrap of white, at least 9″ × 11″, for background
- Scraps of light green, medium green, and red
- Black embroidery floss

Directions

For detailed directions, refer to Paper-Piecing Basics (page 7).

1. Make 3 copies of the pattern (A, B, C).

2. Cut around each segment, adding ¼″ seam allowances.

3. Paper piece each segment.

4. Connect the segments: A to B; A/B to C.

5. Trim ¼″ from the blue line.

6. Hand stitch the nose, and mouth using black embroidery floss.

7. Continue to Snake, Part 2 (next page).

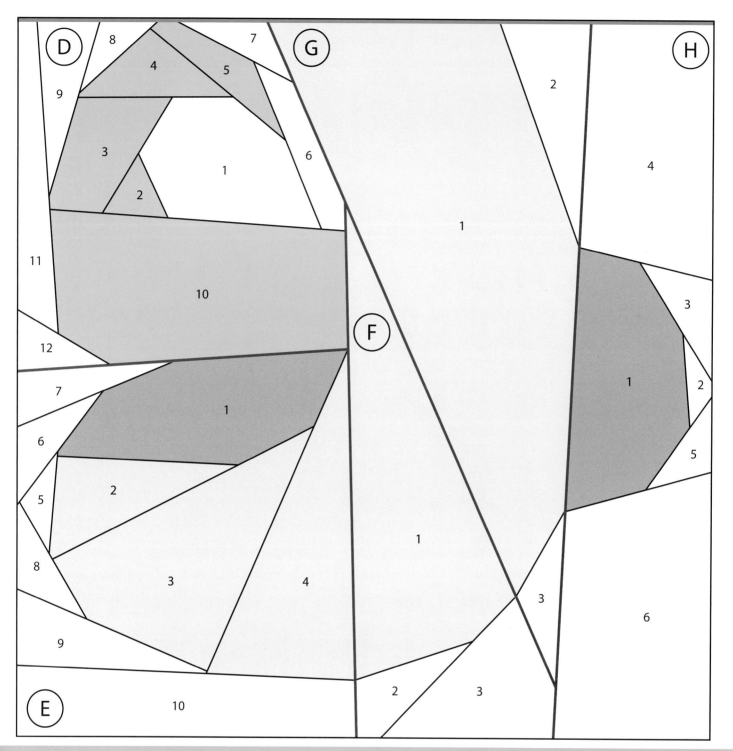

SNAKE, PART 2

Materials

- Large scrap of white, at least 9" × 11", for background

- Scraps of light green, dark green, and darkest green

Directions

For detailed directions, refer to Paper-Piecing Basics (page 7).

1. Make 3 copies of the pattern (D/H, E/G, F).

2. Cut around each segment, adding ¼" seam allowances.

3. Paper piece each segment.

4. Connect the segments: D to E; D/E to F to G to H.

5. Trim ¼" from the blue line. Match and sew Part 1 to Part 2 on the blue lines.

6. Trim the block to 8" × 15½".

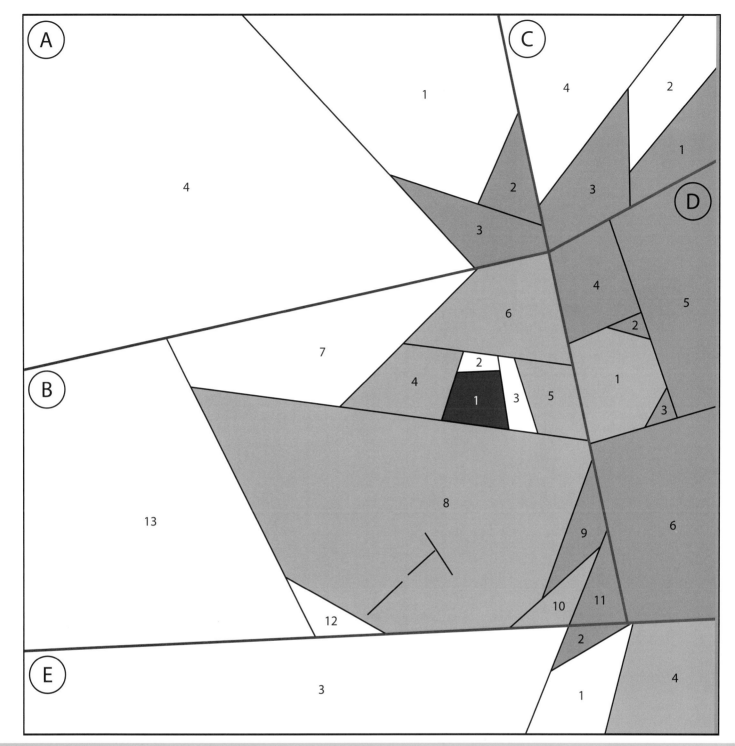

HEDGEHOG, PART 1

Materials

- Large scrap of light blue, at least 9″ × 11″, for background (pictured as white on the pattern)
- Scraps of tan, brown, white, and black
- Black embroidery floss

Directions

For detailed directions, refer to Paper-Piecing Basics (page 7).

1. Make 4 copies of the pattern (A/E, B, C, D).

2. Cut around each segment, adding ¼″ seam allowances.

3. Paper piece each segment.

4. Connect the segments: A to B; C to D; A/B to C/D; A–D to E.

5. Trim ¼″ from the blue line.

6. Hand stitch the mouth using black embroidery floss.

7. Continue to Hedgehog, Part 2 (next page).

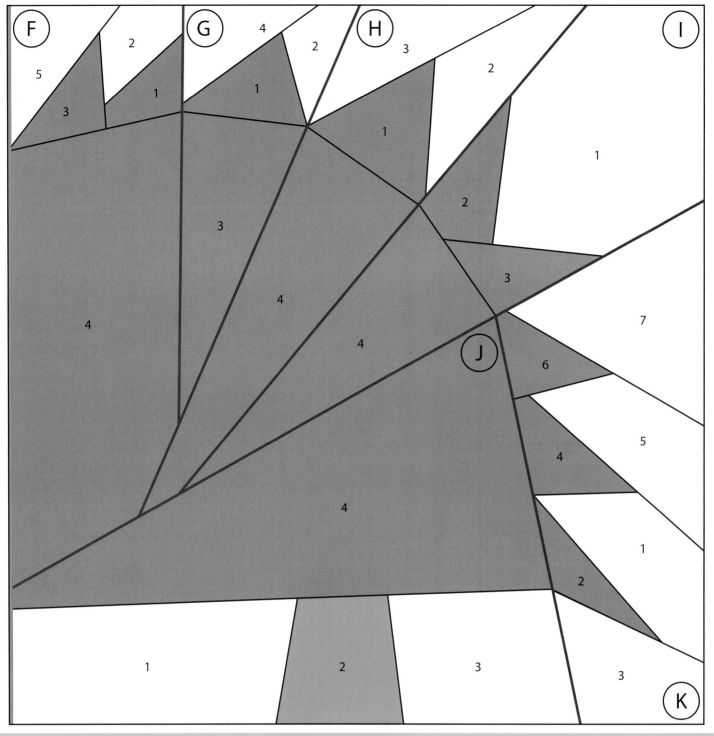

Materials

- Large scrap of light blue, at least 9″ × 11″, for background (pictured as white on the pattern)
- Scraps of tan, and brown

Directions

For detailed directions, refer to Paper-Piecing Basics (page 7).

1. Make 3 copies of the pattern (F/I, G/J, H/K).

2. Cut around each segment, adding ¼″ seam allowances.

3. Paper piece each segment.

4. Connect the segments: F to G to H to I; J to K; F−I to J/K.

5. Trim ¼″ from the blue line. Match and sew Part 1 to Part 2 on the blue lines.

6. Trim the block to 8″ × 15½″.

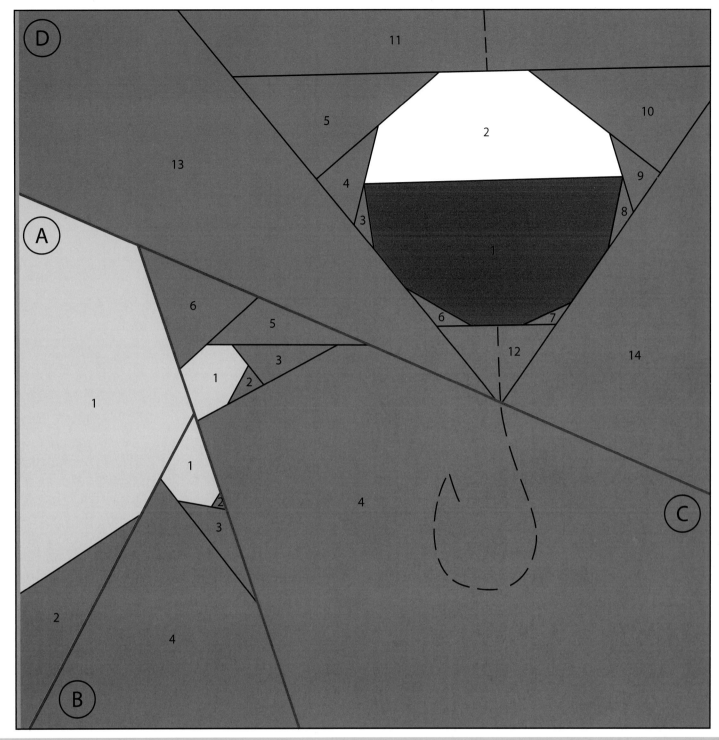

FISH, PART 1

Materials

- Large scrap of aqua, at least 9″ × 11″, for background
- Scraps of green, red, and white
- Black embroidery floss

Directions

For detailed directions, refer to Paper-Piecing Basics (page 7).

1. Make 3 copies of the pattern (A, B/D, C).

2. Cut around each segment, adding ¼″ seam allowances.

3. Paper piece each segment.

4. Connect the segments: A to B to C; A/B/C to D.

5. Trim ¼″ from the blue line.

6. Continue to Fish, Part 2 (next page).

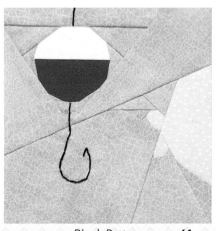

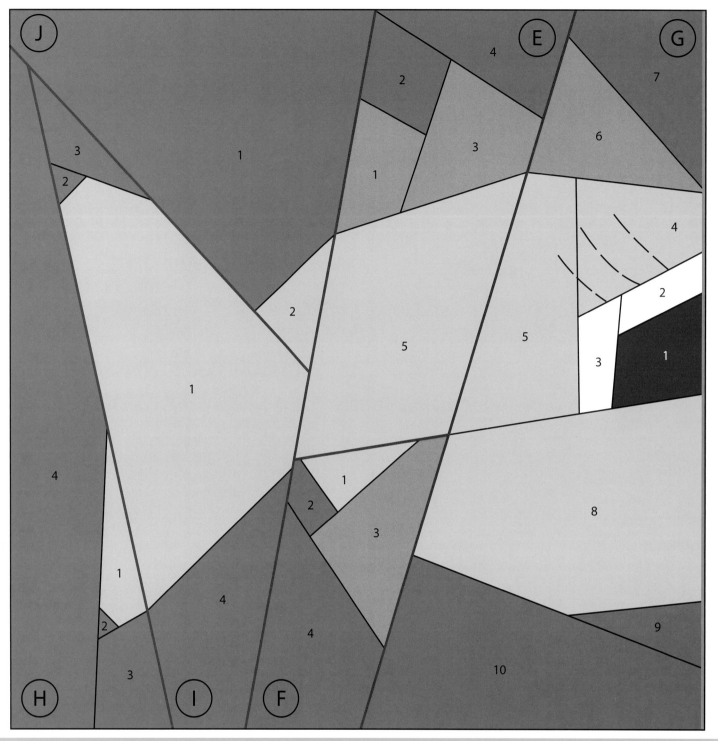

FISH, PART 2

Materials

- Large scrap of aqua, at least 9″ × 11″, for background
- Scraps of black, white, green, and purple

Directions

For detailed directions, refer to Paper-Piecing Basics (page 7).

1. Make 3 copies of the pattern (E/H, G/I, F/J).

2. Cut around each segment, adding ¼″ seam allowances.

3. Paper piece each segment.

4. Connect the segments: E to F; E/F to G; H to I to J; E/F/G to H/I/J.

5. Trim ¼″ from the blue line. Match and sew Part 1 to Part 2 on the blue lines.

6. Trim the block to 8″ × 15½″.

7. Hand stitch the eyelashes, hook and fishing line using black embroidery floss.

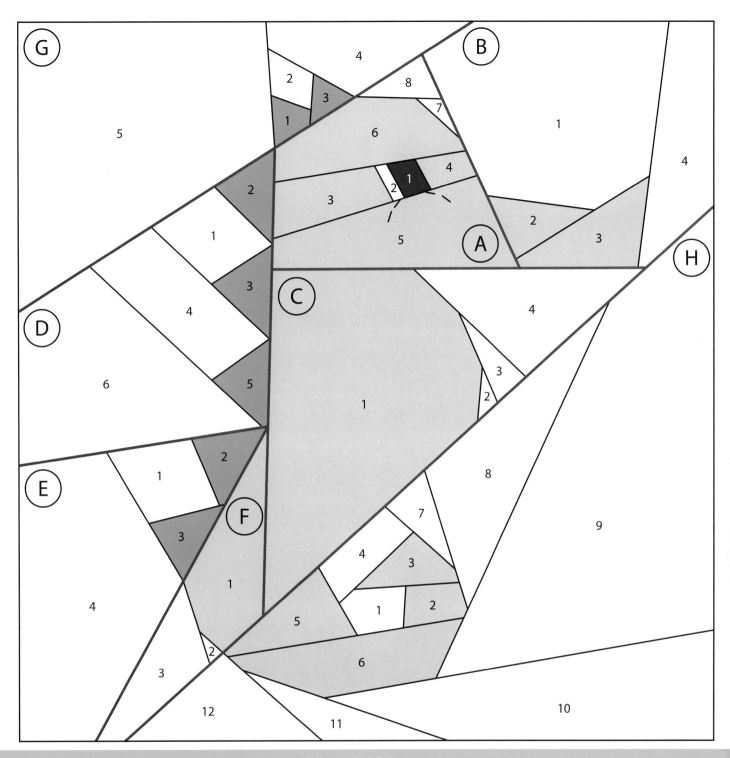

SEAHORSE

Materials

- Large scrap of white, at least 9″ × 11″, for background
- Scraps of light turquoise, dark turquoise, and black
- Black embroidery floss

Directions

For detailed directions, refer to Paper-Piecing Basics (page 7).

1. Make 4 copies of the pattern (A/E/H, B/D, C/G, F).

2. Cut around each segment, adding ¼″ seam allowances.

3. Paper piece each segment.

4. Connect the segments: A to B to C; D to E to F; A/B/C to D/E/F; A–F to G to H.

5. Trim the block to 8″ × 8″.

6. Hand stitch the eye details using black embroidery floss. The pattern shows an embroidered cheek, or add eye lashes, or both!

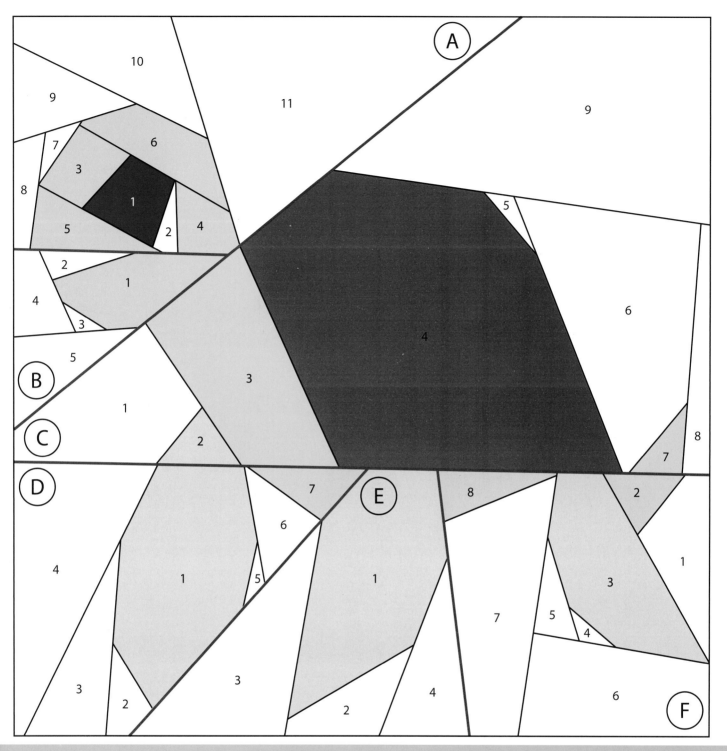

SEA TURTLE

Materials

- Large scrap of white, at least 9″ × 11″, for background
- Scraps of green, turquoise, turtle shell pattern, and black

Directions

For detailed directions, refer to Paper-Piecing Basics (page 7).

1. Make 3 copies of the pattern (A/D/F, B/E, C).

2. Cut around each segment, adding ¼″ seam allowances.

3. Paper piece each segment.

4. Connect the segments: A to B; A/B to C; D to E to F; A/B/C to D/E/F.

5. Trim the block to 8″ × 8″.

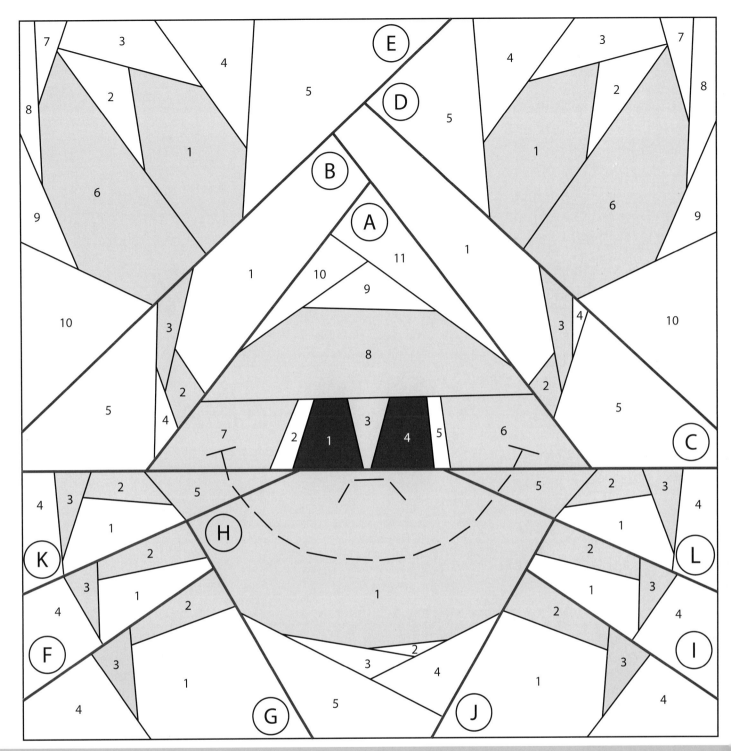

CRAB

Materials
- Large scrap of white, at least 9″ × 11″, for background
- Scraps of turquoise, and black
- Black embroidery floss

Directions
For detailed directions, refer to Paper-Piecing Basics (page 7).

1. Make 4 copies of the pattern (A/D/F/I, B/G/J/L, C/H, E/K).
2. Cut around each segment, adding ¼″ seam allowances.
3. Paper piece each segment.
4. Connect the segments: A to B to C to D to E; F to G; I to J; F/G to H to I/J; F–J to K to L; A–E to F–L.
5. Trim the block to 8″ × 8″.
6. Hand stitch the nose and mouth using black embroidery floss.

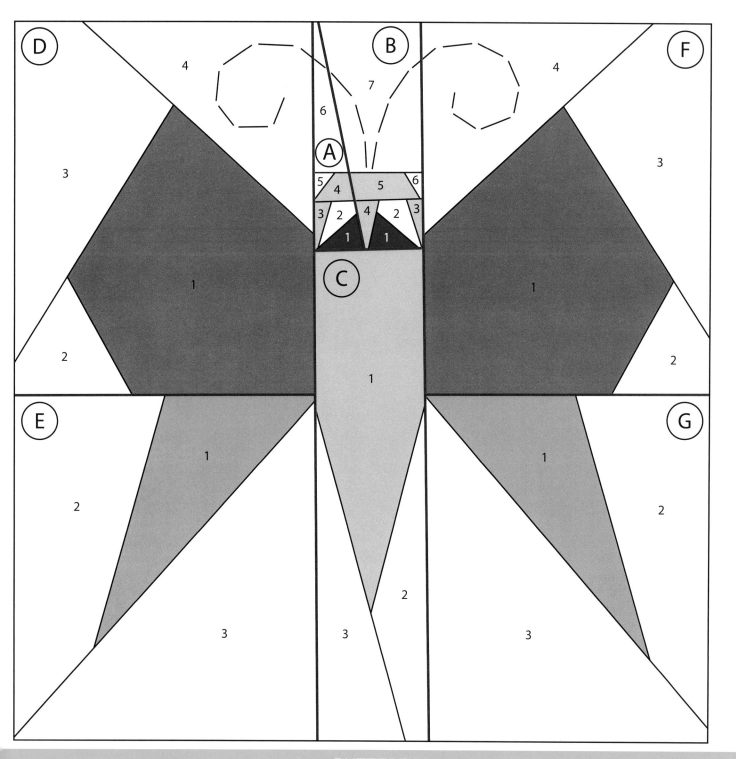

BUTTERFLY

Materials

- Large scrap of white, at least 9" × 11", for background
- Scraps of pink, dark pink, gray, and black
- Black embroidery floss

Directions

For detailed directions, refer to Paper-Piecing Basics (page 7).

1. Make 4 copies of the pattern (A/E/F, B/G, C, D).

2. Cut around each segment, adding ¼" seam allowances.

3. Paper piece each segment.

4. Connect the segments: A to B; A/B to C; D to E; F to G; A/B/C to D/E to F/G.

5. Trim the block to 8" × 8".

6. Hand stitch the antennae using black embroidery floss.

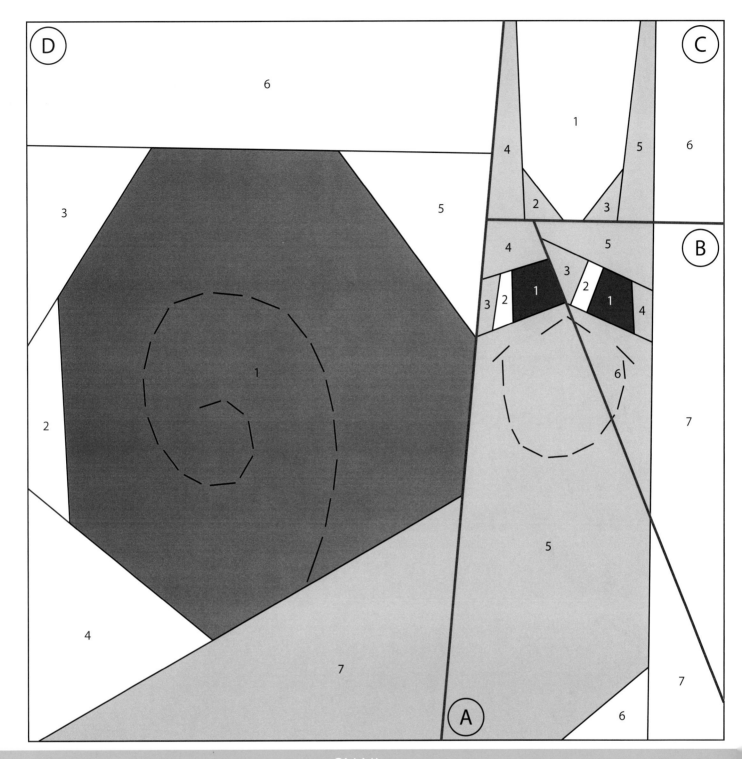

SNAIL

Materials

- Large scrap of white, at least 9″ × 11″, for background
- Scraps of pink, gray, and black
- Black embroidery floss

Directions

For detailed directions, refer to Paper-Piecing Basics (page 7).

1. Make 3 copies of the pattern (A, B/D, C).

2. Cut around each segment, adding ¼″ seam allowances.

3. Paper piece each segment.

4. Connect the segments: A to B; A/B to C; A/B/C to D.

5. Trim the block to 8″ × 8″.

6. Hand stitch the nose, mouth, and shell swirl using black embroidery floss.

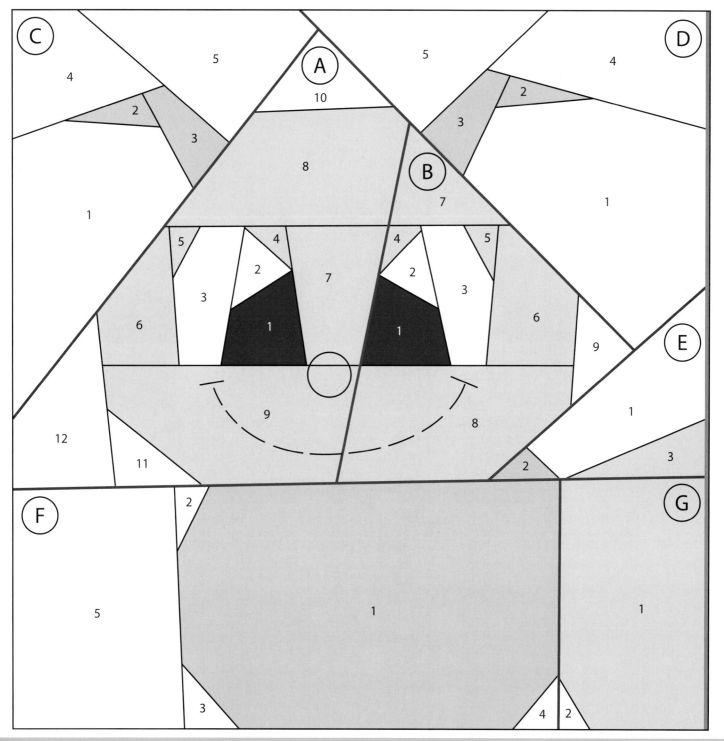

CATERPILLAR, PART 1

Materials

- Large scrap of white, at least 9″ × 11″, for background
- Scraps of green, turquoise, and black
- Black embroidery floss
- Black ½″ button

Directions

For detailed directions, refer to Paper-Piecing Basics (page 7).

1. Make 3 copies of the pattern (A/E, B/C, D/F).

2. Cut around each segment, adding ¼″ seam allowances.

3. Paper piece each segment.

4. Connect the segments: A to B to C to D; A/B/C/D to E; F to G; A/B/C/D/E to F/G.

5. Trim ¼″ from the blue line.

6. Continue to Caterpillar, Part 2 (next page).

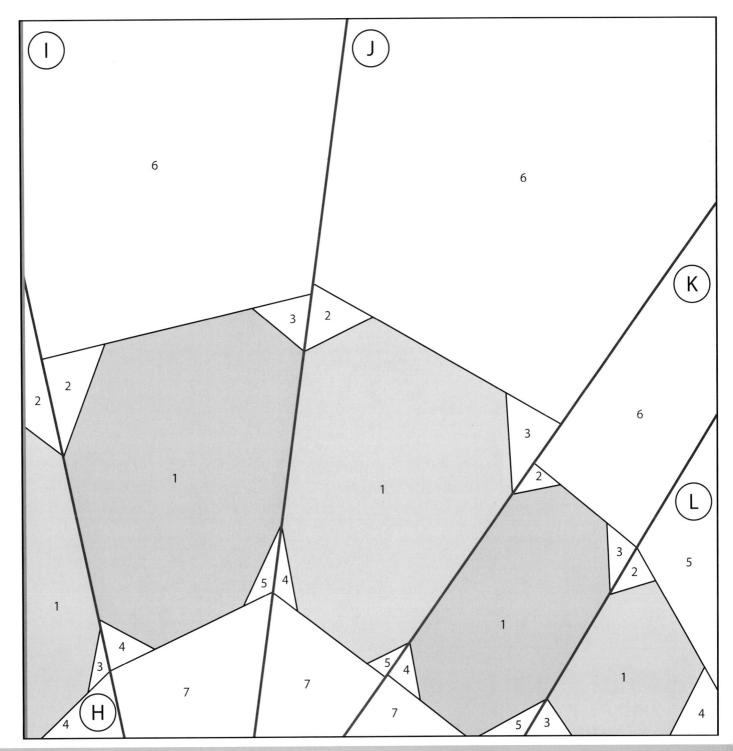

CATERPILLAR, PART 2

Materials
- Large scrap of white, at least 9″ × 11″, for background
- Scraps of green, and turquoise

Directions
For detailed directions, refer to Paper-Piecing Basics (page 7).

1. Make 2 copies of the pattern (H/J/L, I/K).

2. Cut around each segment, adding ¼″ seam allowances.

3. Paper piece each segment.

4. Connect the segments: H to I to J to K to L.

5. Trim ¼″ from the blue line. Match and sew Part 1 to Part 2 on the blue lines.

6. Trim the block to 8″ × 15½″.

7. Hand stitch the mouth using black embroidery floss.

8. Hand sew a black ½″ button for the nose.

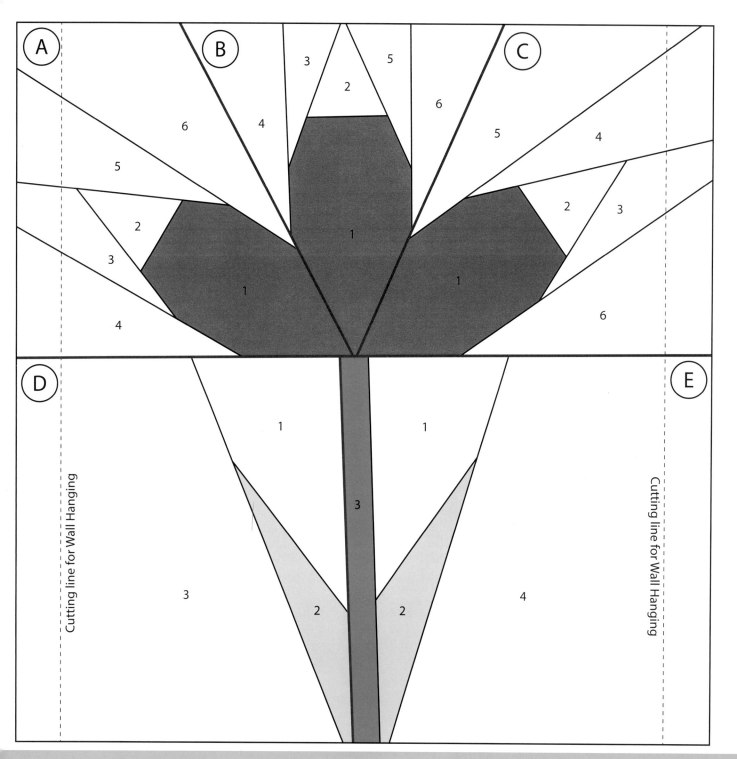

FLOWER

Materials

- Large scrap of white, at least 9″ × 11″, for background
- Scraps of pink, light green, and dark green

Directions

For detailed directions, refer to Paper-Piecing Basics (page 7).

1. Make 5 copies of the pattern (A, B, C, D, E).

2. Cut around each segment, adding ¼″ seam allowances.

3. Paper piece each segment.

4. Connect the segments: A to B to C; D to E; A/B/C to D/E.

5. Trim the block to 8″ × 8″ for a square block; trim to 6½″ wide × 8″ high for the wall hanging.

About the Author

Mary (also known as Marney) Hertel grew up on a small dairy farm in the heart of Wisconsin. Sewing is in her blood, and she likes to say she has "sewn since birth," starting on her mother's sewing machine at a very early age. After securing her art education job straight out of college, she used her first paycheck to purchase a sewing machine. Soon after, she started to quilt and has never stopped.

Mary's favorite method of quilting became paper piecing after she was introduced to this practice in 2013. The puzzle-like quality of paper piecing appealed to Mary and has quickly become her favorite approach to adding an image to a quilt.

Her quirky animal designs are a nod to 35 years of teaching children's art. "I try to keep my animal designs childlike, but expressive," Mary says. She also strives to offer her customers very easy paper-pieced patterns.

Currently, Mary has six previously published books, scores of magazine articles, and over 500 patterns that can be found on Etsy.com, and in many quilting stores throughout the United States.

Enjoy her whimsical designs and her easy-to-paper-piece patterns.

Photo by Gail Cameron

Also by Mary Hertel:

Visit Mary online and follow on social media!

Website: madebymarney.com

Facebook: /madebymarney

Pinterest: /maryhertel

Instagram: @madebymarney

Twitter: madebymarney

Etsy: etsy.com/shop/madebymarney

CREATIVE SPARK
ONLINE LEARNING

Quilting courses to become an expert quilter...

From their studio to yours, Creative Spark instructors are teaching you how to create and become a master of your craft. So not only do you get a look inside their creative space, you also get to be a part of engaging courses that would typically be a one or multi-day workshop from the comfort of your home.

Creative Spark is not your one-size-fits-all online learning experience. We welcome you to be who you are, share, create, and belong.

Scan for a gift from us!